UNABASHED

SELF-ADVOCACY AND THE QUEST
TO FOSTER EMPATHY

BY NIYATI TAMASKAR

Unabashed: Self-Advocacy and the Quest to Foster Empathy
by Niyati Tamaskar

Copyright © 2021

All rights reserved.

This book is a memoir. It reflects the author's present recollections of experiences that occurred in the past. Some names and identifying characteristics have been changed, some events have been compressed, and some dialogue has been recreated.

Paperback ISBN: 978-1-7332245-8-1
E-book ISBN: 978-1-7332245-9-8

DEDICATION

This book is dedicated to my mother.

With courage and conviction,
she inculcated in me the value of standing up for myself.
Empowered, I strive to live
a life unabashed.

PRAISE FOR

UNABASHED: SELF-ADVOCACY AND THE QUEST TO FOSTER EMPATHY

"Widely acclaimed by Forbes magazine as one of the eight books that help **spark human connection in 2020**, Niyati Tamaskar's return following Unafraid doesn't hold back as she challenges our limiting beliefs and urges us to embrace walking in another's shoe. Her personal stories as a woman of color, punctuate survivorship- the time following successful cancer treatment. This book will **empower you** to self-advocate even under the cloud as morbid as the 'C' word, **help educate** how you can be present for loved ones as they navigate their suffering and **help celebrate** the diverse beauty of our backgrounds!"

—Archita Sivakumar Fritz, Host and Producer of *The Nine Oh Six Podcast*, Director of Marketing at a Fortune 300 MedTech Company

"Brave, insightful and vulnerable, Nyati has written a candid part memoir, part guidebook for navigating the cancer care labyrinth, which is often plagued with impossible decisions, heartbreaking news, discrimination and cultural bias. In her second book, Niyati embarks on a personal quest to uncover the formula for human courage and resilience. Her main takeaway? It's OK to not know the whys behind human suffering - an open invitation for anyone willing to reflect on their own fears and prejudices and find the strength to face the unknown with an open heart and empathy."

—Anastasia Ustinova, Journalist, Startup and Innovation Reporter

CONTENTS

1. Introduction 1
2. Baby Girl 13
3. Survivorship Blues 23
4. Reconstruction 35
5. Have Faith 47
6. Parity 55
7. Standing on the Shoulders of Giants 67
8. The Immigrant Story 89
9. Far from Home 105
10. Schooling Then and Now 125
11. Insatiable 139
12. The Pandemic 149
13. A Comedy of Errors 161
14. Stubborn Hope 175

Discussion Guide 183

Acknowledgements 185

Author Bio 187

1. INTRODUCTION

> "Vulnerability is the birthplace of innovation, creativity, and change."
> —Brené Brown

Bright lights, cameras rolling, and a red circle on the stage; *we are going live*! The host introduces the first speaker of the night. I'm behind the curtains, heart pacing. I breathe in through my nose and out through my mouth. I need to calm myself. *Be still my heart; we've got this.*

There's applause, and I find myself walking to the middle of the stage. The lights are so bright that I can barely see the first two rows. But what I do see is my husband, Nuwan; cousins, Vikram and Beena; and nieces, Maya and Arya. I see Gary, PG, Jacob from work, and Dr. McMullen from the Cancer Center. I know other close friends and colleagues are there to see me; I feel their presence in the applause I receive. I am now on stage, about to deliver my first TEDx talk on "Perspective Shift."

Every so often, I run into someone who has not heard of TED talks; *oh, the horror*! TED stands for Technology, Entertainment, and Design and is a nonprofit, nonpartisan foundation dedicated to making ideas accessible. Their tagline is "ideas worth spreading;" their goal is to spark conversation about meaningful topics. TEDx is an offshoot of the larger TED organization. TEDx is targeted to bring the spirit of the global TED talks to local communities throughout the world. If you haven't heard or watched a TED talk, stop right here. You can read my ramblings later; search "TED talks," watch one—any random one—and you will thank me later.

So, back to my TEDx talk. I walk to the middle of the iconic red dot, clicker in hand and microphone taped to my cheek. The microphone is one of those light beige ones that blends with my skin tone. I take a deep breath and start talking. I deliver my 13-minute speech—on the cultural bias and stigma associated with cancer—without wavering. The talk is from my heart. It is moving, sarcastic, and perhaps ironically, funny. I gain trust and let the listeners in, then challenge them. I treat the audience members as my equals, presenting my hypothesis—cancer stigma spans across cultures—and back my claims with research and data. The highlight for me is the closing statement and my call to action, "My name is Niyati Tamaskar, and I'm a year and half into remission. Let's destigmatize cancer together!"

Spoiler alert: I'm a breast cancer survivor.

I receive a roaring standing ovation, someone in the back whistles, and my radiation oncologist, Kevin, runs up to the stage and hands me a bouquet of flowers. My family is misty-eyed from tears of pride.

Hours of practice paid off; the delivery was on point. I nailed it. It was everything I had dreamed about for my first TED experience, and more. Scratch that, it was better than I could have ever imagined.

I had dreamed of becoming a TED speaker, as the pre-cancer Niyati who had no idea of why she would be worthy of the stage. Post-cancer, my perspective changed; I was no longer hesitant about putting myself out there. And the topic was a no-brainer. I wanted to shed light on the taboos surrounding cancer and the universal reach of its stigma. TEDx offered a pedestal upon which to spotlight my message, and once I walked offstage, I knew that I wanted to share my story on larger platforms with a greater reach. This is just the start.

I am often asked about how I made my way to the TEDx stage. Early in 2020, I sought a local event that Nuwan and I could attend for an ideal date night. I found a TEDx talk in Bloomington on "Perspective Shift." When I read the description of this topic, I thought, *who better to speak on this topic than me?* My story seemed practically made for this event: a 34-year-old breastfeeding mother, diagnosed with cancer, goes through a grueling treatment plan, then writes a book about her narrative and the paradigm *shift in perspective* her experience brought.

So, caught up in the moment, without consulting a soul, I filled out an application to be a TEDx speaker, and I clicked send.

If this were a movie, here's how it would go down: event curators would be fighting each other to decide who would get to call me to convince me to head their lineup.

Reality was not so avant-garde. A few days after I applied, I casually told my husband about it. I laughed at myself for being so presumptive to think that they would choose me. Weeks went by, and I all but forgot about it. Other than Nuwan, I hadn't told anyone I'd applied. Meanwhile, a colleague and friend, Kelly, told me about an upcoming speaker opportunity. The Society of Women Engineers (SWE) was gearing up for a global conference, and they issued a call for speakers. "I think you have such a powerful story to share, and you're a natural! You should apply, Niyati," she said. I thought to myself, why not?

Three weeks before the Perspective Shift event, I got a nonchalant e-mail from TEDx Bloomington. My heart skipped a beat as I read, ". . . to see if you might still be interested in presenting. We have an event coming up on March 6, and it is looking like one of six presenters might have to drop out. It would be a tight preparation schedule, but it seems like you've already done a lot of thinking, writing, and talking about your topic, so it might be a good fit. I'd love to chat more!"

Does this mean they want me? I thought. *Because I'll make myself available. I'll clear the calendar, get a sitter, and take time off.* I was a potential backup, which meant that they were considering me as a speaker in case they needed another one as they neared the event date. Before selecting me, they wanted to make sure that I could pull together a speech in three weeks and deliver it without a teleprompter or paper notes. I was up for that challenge. I had a video-call interview with Jen, one of the curators. I proposed three pitches for what I wanted to talk about. In that call itself, gauging Jen's body language and how I was able to pique her interest, I narrowed it down to one theme. *No one wants to hear another cancer tear-jerker story.* I would use the platform to talk about the stigma associated with the c-word. I said to Jen, "Give me a few days. I want to back up my experience and anecdotal information with data." Jen was agreeable.

I hadn't been officially selected yet, but I started researching and refining my talking points. I figured TEDx would be quite selective, and I may not get the opportunity to speak to the larger crowd—but this fact-finding and reflection exercise could help me prepare the application for the SWE opportunity. *No loss.*

Several days passed. I could be described as pitiful with my extreme enthusiasm and desire to be on the TEDx stage. I even started dreaming about the event. I dreamed about being on stage with that iconic red dot, and the roaring applause at the end. Yes, a little pathetic, I know. But this sort of imagining myself in extraordinary situations happens to me often. When I want something desperately, the desire manifests itself in my dreams. Good and bad, my brain plays tricks with me. And maybe those dreams prepare me for the real thing.

TEDx Bloomington did end up selecting me. I know—shocking, right? And I was invited to go to Bloomington for my first in-person practice.

I was quite nervous that day. My mentor, Gary, graciously offered to accompany me to the practice. Sidebar on Gary—he is an empathetic, accessible, salt-of-the-earth man who uses his official work title as Vice President of Power Systems as an enabler for difficult conversations, as opposed to a hierarchical barrier. It was considerate of Gary to give up his Sunday afternoon to provide moral support.

My nerves stemmed from my awareness that the rest of the speakers had a head start in preparing for their respective talks. They were the chosen ones who found out they would be speaking on the TEDx stage three months before the event—unlike me, *the backup* who was chosen three weeks before.

But I think that was the reason why I practiced even harder. I didn't want them to regret or reverse their decision. I was determined to make a lasting first impression.

My first practice was with Gary. The verbal and nonverbal feedback I received from him was enough. The head-nods and chuckles when I was being funny and the display of emotion when I touched on painful moments were right on queue. I was confident that I was on the right path with the speech.

My first practice with the organizing team impressed them enough to give me that spot in the lineup. I was no longer just a backup.

During the three weeks leading up to the talk, I tapped on my resources, confidants, and corporate cornerstones. I consulted with an executive in communications, corporate marketing experts, and my bread and butter: the engineers and leaders who saw me battling cancer. I got brilliant tips on stage presence, body movement, and audience engagement. I also received tips on content and feedback on tone.

During the practice runs I set up, tears were shed. The extraordinary impact I felt in the intimate setting of two or three people made me eager to give my speech to a larger audience. But I shuddered to consider the response I'd get once the live recording was posted online for my family and friends to see. *Would it be too painful to relive my journey?* I wanted to make my family proud, but I feared that any such pride would come with tears.

Over the course of those three weeks, TEDx held practice runs with the lineup of speakers. The curators liked how my talk had evolved and decided to make me the opening act! That's right—from backup speaker to headline act! Of course, I would be disappointed in myself with anything less. The feedback I got from Jen was that she liked the moments of reflection interrupted with levity, and that overall I had an optimistic message.

Everyone loves a cancer survivor, right?

And just like that, a dream turned into reality, and on a crisp Friday evening in March, I delivered my first TEDx talk live on a theater stage. Cheering me on were thirty-some friends and family, with a few hundred others.

•••

After my opening act, I went back into the green room to change out of my ridiculous heels to comfortable slip-ons, and I made my way to my reserved speaker's seat in the audience—set aside for me so I could enjoy the rest of the show. I sat by my lonesome, buzzing from the high of being on stage. I should've been attentive to the next speaker on stage, but instead my mind wandered down memory lane.

I remembered the day of my diagnosis, that fateful Friday morning at 11:10 a.m. when I called the breast health center. How my life changed irrevocably. I recalled the appointment I had with my breast surgeon, the ever-so-kind Dr. Zusan. How her cheeks went red and her eyes welled up when I, in a moment of utter weakness, asked her to *let me die*.

I'm ashamed of that incident.

I remember chemotherapy a little differently now. Somehow, my memories take me to warm blankets, straight from the blanket-oven, that the oncology nurses would wrap around me. I felt so loved.

I have no such fond memories of the double mastectomy. How could I? It was brutal, painful, and like the diagnosis, irrevocable. A part of me was taken away that day on the operating table.

Then came radiation. I also remember this a little differently. According to my first book, there was some crying during sessions. I remember radiation as the last thing in my treatment plan, the final arsenal to decimate the cancer. How naïve I was to think that the end of treatment would mark the closing of that chapter.

The last radiation session left a void in my life; *what do I do now*? And with the soul-searching and book-writing, the answer was clear to me: I need to help women facing their cancer by sharing my story and by making myself available. To listen, without judgement, to their fears and triggers; to be present for them in their darkest moments.

My wandering down memory lane is interrupted as I hear more applause.

The speaker on stage has just finished his talk. My mind snaps back to the present.

During the intermission halfway through the event, I finally get to see my peeps. I kiss Nuwan. Vikram *dada* (dada is a term of reverence attached to older brothers/older male cousins) and Beena give me hugs; Maya and Arya are so proud.

I make my rounds, thanking my friends and colleagues for coming. Lisa, my teammate, says to me, "You are going to change the world."

PG and his wife, Manju, say they are "amazed at how brave I was." PG asks, "How did you memorize all those statistics?"

Pallav, who had helped me during the practice sessions, says, "You did it, Niyati! I really like how you added some spontaneous, unrehearsed bits to the speech." He had heard me deliver my talk a few times in practice and noticed on performance day that I assessed the audience and let my personality shine.

Kruthi and Aiswarya were proud to call me their friend.

It was a memorable evening, made possible by the support and love of an army of friends and my family.

A few months after my TEDx performance, the video was finally available online. I promoted my talk more than I've endorsed my resume or any work experience, wholly because I had a message that I wanted to share with the world—with urgency. Even today, as I write this book, I am contacted by women who are ashamed of their cancer, who can't or choose not to share the diagnosis with their closest friends. Some haven't even told their families. I am helping the women who feel their confidante is a stranger—me!—and who try to find safety, solace, and camaraderie in that.

I hope my TEDx talk can be a catalyst for dialogue; we must rid ourselves of the cancer-curse. In that vein, I texted, e-mailed, called, posted on social media, and further asked others to share the video of my TEDx speech. I reached out to acquaintances coast to coast in the U.S. and Canada. I wrote to my Mexican and Brazilian friends. I e-mailed our former neighbors in the U.K. and several colleagues from England and New Zealand. My family in India, Nuwan's in Sri Lanka and the U.A.E., and friends in Australia and South Korea were all eagerly awaiting the video. The Fortune 500 company that I work for—Cummins—posted an article on the company's intranet with a link to my talk. The organizers of the event were amazed at my enthusiasm and networking.

I didn't think my talk would go viral or anything, but I was hoping to hit a modest hundred thousand views. Cummins alone employs just over 60,000 employees; add that to my network, social media, and friends of friends. I did the math.

The result of all this gusto? Three thousand views of my TED talk over the course of a year. Ha! I love when life shamelessly offers you a reality check. This was my reality check. I still wonder if humanity is tired of *yet another cancer story*. Regardless, the experience was an accomplishment for me, a feather in my cap. My desire to speak before-illness never led to an opportunity. Not for lack of trying, it's just that I was still discovering myself, my message, and my calling. When you go through an utterly harrowing cancer journey, you have a story.

These experiences not only gave me a story, but also focused my intentions: be passionate about helping the distressed while crushing cultural taboos, and you can find your true calling. It's that simple, people.

Something else: once the video was available, I played it for Vihaan, my son, and Aarini, my daughter. It wasn't the *content* that I wanted them to understand, but rather the *concept*:

A woman can be on stage, and that woman is your mother. Your mother has something worthy of saying—something that an audience will pay money to hear. Women can have an opinion and command a call for action.

Yes, I understand that at this point my children were six and three, perhaps not old enough to truly absorb all the lessons I was trying to convey; but I say it's never too early to start. Of course, I want my son to see women in power, but I feel that it is more important for my daughter to see women of color inspire. If ever a time comes when my daughter wonders if she can take on the world, I want her to remember: *Amma* (Amma is mother in parts of South and Southeast Asia) is an electrical engineer, working for a Fortune 500 company, has lived in three continents and worked in two, has published a couple of books, and gives back to society. That is conscientious leadership in action, and I want my baby girl to know she has the backing.

Having young children, however, gives you a lesson in authenticity. I had lofty reasons for wanting my children to watch the TEDx talk. In my mind, I was preparing to hear this from my son, "Wow, Amma, you are amazing! Women can do anything." Instead, it went more like this, "Amma, that's you on the big screen!" He was more surprised that his mother—whom he regularly saw in pajamas and sweatpants and preparing curry in the kitchen—was suddenly on television. Not just any broadcast, but rather a YouTube link: the surefire way to impress kids these days.

Aarini saw the picture of bald-me in the video and said, "Amma have no hair. You were a baby. Now you have hair!" She gets her tenses wrong, but in her three-year-old brain, she observed, reasoned, and reconciled my baldness.

I will never cease to be amazed by how resilient children are. Aarini and Vihaan don't quite recollect the trauma of my illness. And seeing a woman, *their mother*, without hair elicits a simplified explanation.

But I'm getting ahead of myself. The first reality check came to me the night of my event. We got home close to 11:00 p.m. with Vikram dada and family. They planned to spend the weekend with us. After changing into night clothes, I went upstairs to reconnect with my nieces.

I gave the twenty-year old Maya a hard time for laughing so hard that I could pick her out from the crowd. She told me in her defense that she was in splits, because I had said, "My son ran through the door, gave me a hug, and started playing with LEGOs. He didn't even notice I was bald!"

Maya said, "That's our Vihaan, alright."

In that post-TEDx glow, as we chatted in the guestroom, Arya, my nineteen-year-old niece, asked me a tough question: "Why didn't you talk about Aarini in the speech?"

When innocence and honesty challenge your narrative, you know you need to address it. I feebly attempted to answer that question to my nieces' satisfaction. What I said then isn't even clear to me now, because I wasn't prepared to give a meaningful answer at the time. But I spent the next several months self-reflecting: *why have I masked the struggle with Aarini?*

I discovered that there was only one reason I'd avoided bringing her into my speech, or the story of my illness and recovery: it was too hard for me to accept I had *done* this to her. My heart breaks when I think of how unfair my breast cancer was on my baby girl. And this is the trigger to writing a second book, to give justice to my baby girl. *Aarini, my darling, Amma loves you.* Uncovering my trauma and addressing that guilt triggered a chain of events.

How do we navigate cancer after treatment? What does survivorship look like? Better yet, how do we thrive after trauma? Survivorship doesn't feel like freedom, which I thought it would be. It feels like a many-strings-attached lifelong bond.

In hindsight, there are things I wish I had known before treatment. But now that I'm through it, I want to share what I can with you in the hopes that it will help. I want to share the lessons in empathy that my journey taught me.

At every step of this self-awareness, I also pause and think about my children. I want to chronicle my family history, my husband's lineage, and our ancestral narrative—so they know what they are made of.

This book is the fabric of my being; it is the human story—one that I hope to continue unearthing, like peeling the layers of an infinitely sweet and spicy onion. And one that I know will leave you inspired.

2. BABY GIRL

> "The human heart was not designed to beat outside the human body and yet, each child represented just that—a parent's heart bared, beating forever outside its chest."
> —Debra Ginsberg

Aarini was turning one on February 2, 2018, and I had big plans for her milestone birthday. I contacted the local children's museum to see if I could book the whole place for a private event. The earliest availability was in March. *Fine*, I thought. It's a few weeks later than Aarini's birthday, but with weather being decent, I can invite my cousins and their families. This would give us plenty of time to coordinate and plan.

March is a popular month for birthdays in my family. My cousin Apurva's husband, Adam, and their son, Ethan Arjun, are both March-born. My darling nephew, Abir, who lives in India, is also March-born. I wished my family from India could be with us for the celebration as well, but I didn't dwell on that too much, because in mid-March, Nuwan and I had flights booked to take the kids to Dubai, India, and Sri Lanka to visit our parents and siblings. March would be a memorable month—the first birthday of my last-born and a family holiday across the world visiting three countries.

I suggested to Apurva that we should have three cakes, one for each of the children's birthdays: Aarini, Adam, and Ethan. She loved the idea; they would come from Connecticut. My cousins, Prashant and Catharine, and their son, Maadhav from Manhattan, booked their flights, too. The locals—cousins who lived only a few hours away by car—made plans to join the celebration as well. Cousins Deepak and Suzanne from Chicago would come with their daughter, Indrani. Aunts Manda *maushi* (*maushi* means maternal aunt in Marathi) and Shobha *kaku* (*kaku* means paternal uncle's wife) and uncle Yashwant *kaka* (*kaka* means uncle) from Cleveland also planned to come. Vikram dada, Beena, Maya, and Arya firmed up their plans to visit for the big birthday.

Our house would be full of family. I had sleeping arrangements and meals planned. In Indian family gatherings, we congregate and stay under one roof as one big, happy, extended family. There is no talk of getting a hotel; that would be downright disrespectful to the host.

The party was set for Saturday, March 17, and I reserved the local children's museum. The family was abuzz awaiting the event, as we'd all be reunited to celebrate our Aarini.

Aarini's pre-birthday celebration commenced with a cake-smash photoshoot with my friend Amanda, an incredibly talented photographer. The plan was to have pictures printed for Aarini's first birthday party, so people could sign them or write messages for Aarini—something we could read together when she was older and talk about the blessing that she was (and is). The photographs were selected and ordered to print in time for the big day.

Nuwan and I were running errands for the important weekend when I told him how happy I was. "We have our two children, everyone is coming over for the big birthday, and we are going back home to see our parents," I said as he drove. "And honey, the most important thing we have is our health."

I remember that exact moment even today, because in the peak of happiness, I wanted to remind Nuwan, *if we have our health, we have everything*.

Days before our first guest was to arrive—on March 2, amidst all the planning and positivity, love and faith—life took a cruel turn. I was diagnosed with a stage 3C grade 3 invasive ductile carcinoma. Five days before the condemned diagnosis, I felt a lump in my left breast. Since I was breastfeeding, I feared it was the start of mastitis, and I really wanted to get ahead of the impending infection. I'd had mastitis once before, and it was absolutely dreadful. I reported my lump to the OB/GYN's office and got called in for a checkup the next day. I was hoping to walk out of there with a prescription for antibiotics—but instead got a prescription for a mammogram and an ultrasound, scheduled two days out.

I was so annoyed that in the middle of my celebrations and planning, I had to make time for unnecessary procedures. *Just give me the damn antibiotics already.* Mammogram, nerves, ultrasound, tears, biopsy, more tears—all happened on Thursday, March 1. And this brings us to Friday, still completely sure it's not cancer, I wanted to be cut out of my misery. So, I called the breast health center, only to get positively launched into a nightmarish scenario. "All three sites have tested positive for cancer."

I reminisce about the time I thought mastitis was "absolutely dreadful."

Painfully but almost immediately, I called and informed my family of the devastating news. Knowing that we were not in a position to host or celebrate—and that my treatment needed to start right away—my cousins cancelled their travel plans, joined me in the absolute shock of my diagnosis, and asked me how they could help and when they could come over. I canceled the cake order and forgot to cancel the museum booking, but that didn't matter. We were in the middle of coordinating my treatment plan with my oncologist, breast surgeon, and plastic surgeon. I had my first chemo cycle two days before Aarini's birthday party celebration.

And just like that, my baby girl didn't have a first birthday party.

The night I was diagnosed, Nuwan and I lay in bed—shell-shocked. I was co-sleeping with Aarini, because it was so much easier to breastfeed that way. She was in the middle of the bed, nuzzled up against me. The night was eerily quiet. I could hear Aarini suckling—and my heart thumping so hard I could feel it in my ears. I knew I had only a few more days of feeding Aarini on the non-cancerous side. When she turned one, we had introduced her to cow's milk, but she preferred nursing over drinking bottled milk. And that was OK with me; I was in no rush to wean her. But now I had mere days to figure out how to cut her off cold turkey.

My thoughts ran amok. *The co-sleeping needs to stop. If she can smell me, she will want my milk. How do you explain this to a one-year-old?*

Within a few days of my diagnosis, my mother came from India. She closed up her home, took an indefinite leave of absence from work—she dropped everything. She took the next available flight from Mumbai to Indianapolis, flew some twenty-two hours, and showed up at my doorstep.

We had a massive battle ahead of us, and my mother was there to help us.

I'll give you the abridged version of my journey: seven cycles of dose dense chemotherapy followed by a double mastectomy and removal of seven lymph nodes to finish strong (translate broken) after the twenty-eight sessions of breath-hold technique radiation.

I handed my mother the role of co-sleeping with Aarini. And that's how we weaned her. If Aarini cried at night, my mother and Nuwan would take turns soothing her and giving her cow's milk. When she would see me, there were tears of betrayal glistening in her dark eyes. Aarini could not comprehend why I wouldn't feed her.

Under normal circumstances—you know, with breastfeeding mothers not diagnosed with breast cancer—most of us still feel guilty when we wean our babies. But commonly, we give in, feed a little, and try to ease the transition. I had Vihaan's weaning process fresh in my mind. We had done it in phases: stopped daytime nursing first but still breastfed at night. Sometimes I would give in when we would pick him up from daycare. It was a common and routine negotiation with a two-year-old.

If this were the two-year mark with Aarini, I wouldn't feel so terrible. But it wasn't.

You might reason: well, it's more important for you to be alive and healthy than to anguish over breastfeeding. But that's the thing, right? Cancer takes away so much. This was one more piece of my life—our lives—it had claimed.

Cancer invaded my dreams, turning them into nightmares. Seeing my young children broke my heart, because I had so much love to give—so much more to do, to raise them into upstanding citizens of society, into caring human beings. It broke my heart to think, don't they deserve a healthy mother?

I read a statement by Geoff Eaton, who is executive director of Young Adult Cancer Canada, which echoed my struggle, "The reality of having to face the possibility of your death way sooner than you were expecting is a lot more intense when you have children." Everything I was feeling seemed orders of magnitude greater, because I was a mother of toddlers.

Aarini is a sensitive child who wanted me to nurse her, but she quickly realized if she wanted me to hold her, she would need to accept the bottle. My sweet baby girl was eager to compromise, because her need for her Amma trumped her need for breastmilk. That level of maturity from a one-year-old is not what I wanted. I would much rather have Aarini behave like other one-year-olds—unreasonable, adorable, and the center of the universe.

The center of our universe became my cancer, not my child—my cancer, and how I needed to beat it.

I took tremendous comfort and drew strength from providing Aarini with the physical comfort she longed for. Her snuggles and kisses were my oxygen. Unfortunately, the physical connection would be temporarily halted after my upcoming surgery.

The stress of managing the household—while watching me lose my hair and battle the symptoms of chemotherapy—took a toll on my mother. She decided to return to India, and my sister, Priya, took her place.

Priya left her newborn daughter and toddler son with her husband, Kamlesh, and her in-laws to come and help us. If you open my dictionary to look for the meaning of love, sacrifice, loyalty, and compassion, you will only find one word: *Priya*. I am blessed that way.

Something incredible happened when Aarini saw Priya for the first time: she assumed it was me! My sister and I look alike. And at that point in my life, Priya looked more like me than I did, because she had hair. Besides causing Aarini to think Priya was me, my sister tricked my phone as well; my smartphone that unlocks with facial recognition unlocked consistently with my sister's face! So, both phone and Aarini took to Priya like a mother. And for a brief while, my baby girl had two mothers.

Priya co-slept with Aarini, and the whole house worked like a well-oiled machine. It was bittersweet, because I missed my baby nuzzled next to my body at night. Co-sleeping with Aarini (as I'd done with newborn Vihaan), I slumbered to the rhythm of her breathing. A cough, a hiccup, a fast breath, and I'd wake right up. Now with Aarini sleeping with my sister, I felt alone. It didn't help that the cancer made me feel so alone. But you know how parents say they would take a bullet for their child? Here's me saying I would let my breastfeeding, co-sleeping infant sleep away from me, if that meant an easier experience for her. It wasn't easy for me; it was necessary.

On July 12, 2018, I had my double mastectomy and lymph node dissection. The English language is limited in its vocabulary to fully describe the physical pain and mental anguish I suffered after this surgery. The pain was debilitating. It was a five-and-a-half-hour surgery, followed by a one-night stay in the hospital. Dictated by insurance, I was to be in the hospital for less than one day, technically twenty-three hours. Going home seemed premature, but staying in the hospital was a demeaning experience—thanks to an uncaring nurse—so I was ready to return home.

The forty-five-minute car ride from the surgery center to my home was excruciating. Every bump in the road felt like a punch in the chest. And this was with narcotics and a local anesthetic pump inserted by the plastic surgeon.

I couldn't lift either of my arms. I didn't have the strength to lift a spoon. Priya spoon-fed me when we got home. That's how horrible it was.

In all of this, I had two children under four wanting to be with their Amma.

Nuwan explained to Vihaan, "Amma has got an ouchie, OK, Vihaan? We must let Amma rest. When you want to go close to Amma, go to her legs and feet. OK, Vihaan? We don't go close to Amma's arms." A lot of affirmations later—Do you understand, Vihaan? No touching Amma other than her legs; and we let her rest—there was some level of comprehension. Vihaan's brain processed this as well as a four-year-old's could. He took to stroking my legs, or if I was sitting on the couch, playing by my feet. I told him he could give me kisses on the cheek gently.

But Aarini, at her age, did not know how to be gentle. When she approached my face, she'd have both arms out, ready to grab my neck. And when she saw me, she wanted me to pick her up. But picking her up was not possible, and even having her on my lap was out. Anywhere close to my amputated chest was painful and extremely sensitive. That first cough after a double mastectomy, Lord have mercy, was brutal.

So, we had to keep some distance. Priya engulfed her with love and kisses. But the child was acutely aware that she was being kept away from me. And the heart wrenching wails Aarini vocalized to express the injustice in her life haunted my dreams.

This was the time I lost faith in myself as a mother. *Was I causing more harm than good by even being in the house?* Aarini suffered as she endured our separation. My sister was weeks away from heading back to India. Priya suggested that I let her take Aarini back to Mumbai with her. My mother seconded that idea. They assured me they would give her so much love and attention, and that once I was done with radiation, my mother would bring her back. *Jijaji* (*Jijaji* is a term of respect used for brother-in-law in Hindi) got a whiff of the discussions and immediately jumped on board. Kamlesh didn't hesitate for a second to agree to care for another baby.

I gingerly asked Nuwan his thoughts, sensing his reaction. Nuwan said, "We can't send Aarini away. We will get through this together as a family." I let it rest.

I broached the topic with Manda maushi. She encouraged me, saying we were going through so much. "Aarini already thinks Priya is her mother; why don't you send her?" she asked. "It's just a matter of a few months, and she won't remember a thing."

I asked my cousin, Catharine, and she told me to do what felt right.

It actually felt right to send Aarini to Mumbai. Priya loves her like her own, and my brother-in-law had a heart of gold and would take care of Aarini. My mother would resume co-sleeping, because she loved having a little one by her side. And Kamlesh's parents love little children; Kamlesh's mother would dote on her.

But the idea still felt uncomfortable, somewhere deep down, and I was torn. I asked Nuwan to reconsider, but he would have none of it; there was no way he would send Aarini away for months. He wouldn't dream of parting with either of the children, even for a weekend.

So, that was it for me—the deciding factor. I went with Nuwan's wishes.

In hindsight, I am so grateful that I listened to Nuwan, and we persevered. I would've regretted sending Aarini away from me. I am dealing with so much guilt as it is, sending my baby to India is something I would have struggled to grapple with for years to come, if not for the rest of my life.

Strangely, this is what I wish for any young mother with cancer: I hope you have family who will move mountains for you, who will offer to take your child, who will leave their baby behind to take care of yours. I am blessed with a family that not only sticks together, but also shows up. My family was with me, and that is my wish for anyone going through a life-altering diagnosis.

When I wrote *Unafraid* about my breast cancer journey, this part of my story was too painful to talk about. I didn't want to write about Aarini's screams—or how I contemplated sending her away for a couple of months. Above all, I felt guilty.

A mother's guilt is so deep and fundamental in nature that it can even make an extrovert like me shut down. I put these memories in a tiny box, locked the box in another box, and shelved it in a deep corner of my heart. It wasn't till my nieces asked me on the night of my TEDx—"Why don't you talk about Aarini and how hard it was?"—that I realized I was doing myself and Aarini a disservice.

In the soul-searching process of writing this chapter, I realized something else. Somewhere deep in my subconscious, the struggle over reconciling my guilt manifested itself on the book cover of *Unafraid*. Of all the cover designs I worked on with my designer, Asya, the one that appealed to me was that illustration of a mother with long, wavy hair caressing her baby, which was code for me breastfeeding Aarini.

Aarini had a bit of separation anxiety as she got older. Most children develop some form of it at around the eighteen-month mark. And in normal circumstances, this would not have concerned me much. But by now, we all know I no longer had the luxury of normal circumstances. I blame the cancer, my treatment, the abrupt weaning, the weeks I couldn't hold her, and the days I spent more time asleep than awake because of debilitating fatigue. I am convinced I had caused this child's separation anxiety.

Everything I view is through cancer-tinted glasses—literally the opposite of rose-colored glasses. The separation anxiety is better now, but even at age four, Aarini prefers me over anyone else—and will also treat Nuwan as an enemy of the state if she doesn't get access to me. It has not been easy on her little brain to understand that we are post-treatment, and she has me now.

As for me, I give in—totally and wholly—to my baby girl. There are times I get judged for that. Comments like, "She is too used to you; she needs you all the time," are not completely unwarranted but I seal my lips. I will give whatever it takes to restore Aarini's sense of security. I hope that someday, when she is old enough, she will ask questions and want to see photographs of her earliest years. I want to show her that even in the hardest of times, we were an unbroken family unit. And that I'll always be her Amma.

3. SURVIVORSHIP BLUES

> "A ship is safe in harbor, but that's not what ships are for."
> —John A. Shedd

I finished my cancer treatment on October 3, 2018, after my twenty-eighth session of radiation. I was free, released into normalcy. No daily visits to the cancer center, no bi-weekly touching base with my oncologist, no scans, no tests. No more doctor's appointments in the near-term future. I was scheduled to have my first follow-up in January 2019. And thus starts my story—and struggle with survivorship.

I thought ringing the bell to commemorate the end of treatment would be a celebration. But I felt numb. I was beaten up, my body was disfigured, and my hair was sprouting back, but still patchy.

I imagined this is what it must feel like after a traumatic event. Dr. McMullen (Kevin) and Dr. Wagner (Stephanie) told me they were there for me, and to contact them if I needed anything—text, call, get an appointment at the cancer center. They had my back. But I felt a void. How do you go from fighting for your life—to sitting in a conference room discussing engine controls? For all the literature around chemotherapy, and forums on symptoms, where is the Guide to Survivorship? For the army of people that rallied around me during treatment, who should I call on now that I am done with treatment? I was certain that the end of treatment would be a celebration, but why didn't it feel like one?

Labeling these feelings as post traumatic shock syndrome can surely make the therapist's job easy, but I would like to argue that it is not that simple. I feel the most vulnerable in remission, and I hate that feeling.

I am hesitant to celebrate too much, to be too happy, to laugh too loudly. That is not to say I sit around sulking, moping, or crying. It is worse. I am happy, I laugh, I celebrate my kids' milestones; but I wonder if I am tempting fate. Do I deserve to feel happiness and unadulterated joy post-cancer? I know this is superstition rearing its ugly head, but these preconceived notions are ingrained in me.

Part of my lifelong survivorship journey will be blemished with guilt; I am acutely aware of that. And this is not just survivor's guilt; this is a mother's guilt. As an Indian mother, I want to claim that our mother's guilt runs deeper and stronger than in any other culture.

Speaking of celebrations, in a feeble attempt to cope with the guilt of not having a one-year birthday party for Aarini, I threw a massive second birthday party. We rented out the local museum, as we meant to do for her first birthday. More than fifty children attended, along with their parents. Our dear friends, Miguel and Raquel, flew in from Florida with their son, Leo, to celebrate with us. The second birthday was everything I had hoped it would be.

As the months rolled on after the end of treatment, weighty dates made their way through the calendar. March 2—the day I was diagnosed; March 14—the start of chemotherapy; July 12—my double mastectomy and lymph node dissection; October 3—the end of treatment, my first day in remission. While some dates are more painful than others, March 2 will forever be tarnished. How do I acknowledge the date? I could pretend it means nothing, but it does! I could spend the day crying. That's a rubbish option; I'm better than that. I could celebrate that we beat it. But celebrating seems wrong; there's nothing celebratory about the memory of that date. I would love for someone to tell me what to do, an authentic Survivorship Guide, not one of those trite 'I'm thankful for the lessons that cancer has taught me' books. I want something to show me the gritty parts of how to live after feeling the skirt of death.

Since I can't find such a guide, I'm writing my own, of sorts. Bear with me, as I'm living it while I write.

In the unformulated life of a survivor, there is one thing that has greatly helped me: to know that other survivors feel the same, and that I am not alone in my confusion. My recommendation to fellow survivors is to go find your tribe. The good thing is that this concept applies to other situations, too. I have a friend who went through a trying IVF process. While she didn't share her journey with the rest of us, she found another woman going through the same trials. They found solace in each other. It was only after she delivered her beautiful baby boy that she shared her story. I respect her courage; you must do what's right for you. Finding a tribe can make the journey more manageable.

Also, feel free to be fierce about not letting people into your tribe. It might sound cruel, but hear me out, please. I am on a breast cancer forum where a woman who is four years into remission claims she has forgotten about her cancer. Why then is this troll on a cancer forum? The internet and its gems. I hereby give you permission to be selective about your clanswomen.

Something that still bothers me is the advice to "just be positive." Casually asking a person who has faced cancer—or, let's say, lost a parent, miscarried a child, been on the frontlines of war, lost all their possessions to a natural disaster—to just be positive is callous. It brushes off their trauma.

Most survivors will attest that we crave validity. When I speak to fellow cancer patients, I acknowledge their fears and authenticate their anxiety. I painfully reminisce about my feelings, so they know they are not alone. During treatment, I felt isolated at times. So, it became my mission to state out loud to other patients, "You are not alone." I have written that in my letters and notes to patients. I hope the women I've had the honor of supporting feel a bit less lonely.

Something that has significantly helped my mental well-being is finding ways to support, mentor, and be there for other cancer patients. All the kindness, love, support, and meals I received during my treatment made me realize the only way I could pay my friends and colleagues back is to pay it forward. And those interactions, visits to the infusion center, offering my shoulder to a woman so she could cry her heart out, or listening with my head lowered as a grown man broke down about his wife's diagnosis—those situations are my calling.

My core group is adolescents and young adults, also known as AYAs in the cancer world. Find me a minority AYA lady, and I'm all over that. Most of the AYA minority women I've had the honor of supporting have been introduced to me through the cancer center. Others have contacted me after reading *Unafraid*. I am on a few online forums where I get to virtually connect with women still in treatment and other survivors. Helping cancer survivors is where I am validated. When I was a sounding board for a young Indian mother who was diagnosed with an aggressive form of breast cancer, I felt my purpose in life was getting revealed to me.

I am not saying it is all peachy for me, or that I'm even-keeled or in Zen mode when someone shares their news. I have my own struggles behind the scenes. My heart breaks when recently diagnosed women talk about their children. I am reminded of the dark period in my life. I get angry at the universe when I notice how common breast cancer has become in the younger age group, and I feel disheartened when it hits a young mother. I met a woman who was diagnosed with brain cancer while she was pregnant. She survived, as did her baby, and she is doing well in remission. But brain cancer while pregnant is cruel. Back to my gripe with the English language, *cruel* doesn't begin to describe my feelings about cancer when pregnant.

I get frustrated when cancer patients are hesitant to ask questions of their medical care teams. It is imperative to be a self-advocate when dealing with cancer treatment. I reiterate that in my books and speaking, but sometimes the women I am helping lack the confidence or courage to ask questions of their medical teams. I argue, "You have the courage; you are going through cancer treatment! You have more strength than a healthy person sitting next to you. Use that courage to voice your symptoms and ask those burning questions!" Sometimes I wish I could be present in oncology appointments to be the patient's advocate.

If you are wondering: Why do you put yourself through this? Are you a glutton for punishment? The answer is no, because while supporting recently diagnosed women, I am shrouded in my own doubts and worries. Recurrence, long-term survival, quality of life, bone density, hemoglobin levels, hormones . . . I could go on. Survivorship is not easy. But my existence is made worthy when I can help another navigate through their storm. Doubts about my body and my health are put into perspective—and the worry is put on the back burner, on a low simmer.

Survivorship is messy. There are triggers. And from speaking to survivor sisters, I know now that I am not alone in this aspect either. In the past two years, whenever I have heard about a celebrity dying of cancer, I have found myself asking Nuwan the same question, "With all the resources and access to top doctors and cancer centers . . . how did Chadwick Boseman still die of cancer?" Before my cancer diagnosis, when famous people died of the disease, it didn't shake my world or my belief system. For example, when Steve Jobs succumbed to pancreatic cancer, I thought it was a terrible loss. But I didn't go into Google-search mania to dig up cancer details, staging, and treatment. It was simply *sad news*. Now, it is different. Celebrity cancer death is a trigger, and I can't resist the urge to find out more. In my warped mind, I have negotiated a deal. If I don't have the exact cancer type and staging, it won't happen to me. I know that's not how cancer works, but this is how coping looks.

One group of people I feel I haven't been able to help adequately are the ones with stage IV disease. Stage IV is considered terminal, but studies show that even those with stage IV can live for many years. During my diagnosis, I prayed and asked my sister to pray strongly that I didn't have stage IV. Because in my mind, that was a death sentence. And the certainty of death seemed like too much to bear, despite it being the only certainty of life—for *all* of us. I was wrong in my extreme view about stage IV. Cancer staging and lifelines are not so black and white. But the problem is, I had that view, and now I feel like a phony when a stage IV patient is introduced to me. I lend a sympathetic ear, but I wonder how can I pretend to know how hard such a diagnosis is? I wonder what the quality of life is at stage IV—with anxiety and uncertainty. All other stages I can relate to; I don't have to fake it. I can be authentic.

Another group of survivors my heart breaks for is childless women who won't be able to have children in the future because of their cancer and treatment plans—sometimes it's a hysterectomy, other times it is hormonal suppression. The world of fertility and desire to have children is a personal and sensitive journey for most women. Even women who choose not to have children are judged. In this arena, being robbed of the possibility of conceiving as a trade-off for staying alive is harsh. I feel a pang of guilt when I know women who cannot bear children read my first book, because I talk at such length about how my world changed for the better when I had children—and how my monkeys helped me through my journey. I feel terrible thinking that there are cancer survivors who don't have that option.

Speaking of conceiving, I had a scheduled follow-up with my OB/GYN neighbor and dear friend, Degaulle, post cancer-treatment. While we were talking ovaries and uterus linings, things we need to watch, he jokingly said, "I'll kick your butt if you get pregnant again!" The man whose sole business is *to deliver babies*—yes, I am choosing to ignore all other unpleasant parts of obstetrics and gynecology that make up his profession: ectopic pregnancies, emergency hysterectomies, ovarian cysts, and all. Degaulle's job, in my utopian yearning, is preggo women and delivery. So, as I claim, a man whose business is to bring babies into this world is telling me not to be with child again.

A week later, I had a follow-up with my radiation oncologist. I told Kevin, "During the discussion with Degaulle, he said he would . . . and I quote . . . *kick my butt* if I got pregnant again."

Kevin burst out laughing, "We would all kick your butt if you got pregnant."

I'm sorry, is this my reality? I am being forbidden, or in kinder words, "heavily discouraged" from having another child? I was not told this explicitly during my diagnosis. Maybe this is something all pre-menopausal women should assume if they have endured cancer treatment. But no one told me point-blank that my childbearing days were over.

Before I lament, let me level set. I have always wanted two children—no more, no less. Back home, educated Indians look down on couples with more than two kids. Among the literate and elite, it is common to stop at one child—one and done. Two kids is a crowd, and more than two is sacrilege. There is a national emphasis on controlling overpopulation. We are taught from an impressionable age, *Hum do humare do,* which translates into "us two, our two." Lack of education or no access to birth control tends to be the root cause of these large families. Our live-in maid was a mother of five, and that is a common trend. Educated Indians also look down on religions that preach relentless procreation as a means for furthering the religion. While it might have been an effective tool in the ancient era, to continue the same sentiment now, when there are seven billion people on Earth, seems out of date.

Alright, so this is a long, drawn-out explanation of why I wanted only two children; in short, I was programmed that way.

With this background, when my OB tells me he'll kick my butt and Kevin seconds that, you would assume this aligns with my already-ingrained idea of my ideal family structure. But sigh, what do you think happens when I'm told not to do something? I want to do it. (Note for future interactions with me, reverse psychology works like a charm.) Telling me *not* to have children planted a desire in me *to* have another child!

While I only joked about it at my follow-ups, my subconscious went into breeding mode. And I started to dream about being pregnant for a third time. I dreamed about welcoming a child into this world, and I couldn't stop my subconscious, so the only thing my conscious self could do is joke about it.

Humor is my coping mechanism; I don't claim it's healthy.

I was texting Degaulle about a mid-life crisis, and I told him: "I cannot decide between a tattoo and having a baby."

His frantic text back: "Niyati! Get a tattoo! Get a hundred tattoos!"

I laughed. He might have thought I was serious. Actually, I was just coming to terms with the fact that more children were no longer in the plan, even though that was never my plan. My moment of sweet neurosis!

I want to pause here and circle back to childless cancer survivors, whom I have attempted to support, who cannot bear children after the damn cancer. If my subconscious played so heavily on *no-more-children for me*, how do these women cope? What dreams haunt their night's rest? I'm astounded that my programming of only-two children wavered post-cancer. Are there women in the group who feel a similar quiver once they are told not to get pregnant?

I can never fully know these answers, and this is not a topic I would initiate in a discussion. I am not equipped, because all I could say is, "Life is not fair." And, "I'm sorry that biological children are not an option."

I do, however, have enough sense to not suggest, "You can always adopt." More on adoption advice coming up.

•••

As a survivor, I am hyper-aware of my body. I notice the smallest of changes; the slightest of tingles has me on alert. And I communicate that to my cancer center team, which is mentally taxing and time-consuming.

One particularly dreary morning, my teammate Lisa and I decided to carpool to the office. That afternoon when I got in the car, as I was zipping up my jacket, I felt a lump on my throat. My heart sank, my face got hot, and my legs felt numb. And I was the one driving. I kept touching this lump to see if I was imagining it. It was very much there. Lisa was talking about work, but I couldn't follow what she was saying. My mind was elsewhere. I needed to call the cancer center and get an appointment to get this looked at. It was going to be about twenty minutes till we got to

Lisa's place. I was palpitating. I finally broke down and told Lisa I needed to make a call. My phone was connected to my car's Bluetooth, so sweet Lisa could hear the recipient.

"Cancer Center, how many I help you?"

"Hi, this is Niyati Tamaskar [date of birth] . . . I would like an appointment with Dr. McMullen please, at the earliest availability." The cancer center nurses know me, so that helps a lot when I call.

The nurse asked, "What can I say is the reason for the appointment?"

I fibbed and told the nurse that "Dr. McMullen is aware."

I apologized to Lisa for the phone call, but she could sense the quiver in my voice, and gave me space. While I was in Lisa's driveway, I texted Dr. McMullen that I'd found a lump on my throat and made an appointment to see him. He asked me to send him a picture of my throat. I took a picture and sent it.

The next day, Nuwan and I both went to the cancer center. Kevin—since we are on a first name basis—did a physical evaluation and ordered a CT scan for the following day. He said he would talk to me right after the CT, and that he would have the CT read stat. You see, waiting and not knowing is the worst part. The anxiety has caused my heart to age a decade, I reckon! Or *scanxiety*, as I like to call it. I was appreciative that Kevin pushed to get my results read swiftly. The next day, we went in for my CT and waited for the results. Kevin had us checked into an examination room. He waltzed through the door, cheerful as ever, and said, "Niyati, I've just read your CT; everything is fine." We felt a rush of relief.

The lump was still there, of course. I asked him, "Then what is this lump?"

He said, "I'm not sure. Could be a trauma." It was reddened from my touching it incessantly. "Observe it over the next couple of days, and keep me informed."

Days went by—and the bump, not lump, so it seemed—subsided. I texted Kevin when the bump was no longer palpable. He was pleased that this chapter was over.

A few months later, I had a similar scare. Just below my collar bone on the right side, I felt something. I repeated the exercise. Kevin did an examination and said to me in a grave, concerned voice, "That, Niyati, right here, do you feel it?" I nodded vehemently, "That is your rib." I felt so stupid. But determined to save face, I argued that I couldn't feel said *rib* on my left side. Kevin then gave me an anatomy lesson, and behold, I had that rib on the left, too! I had no further questions. Let's just say that wasn't my finest moment.

The problem is, while I am cancer-free based on the pathologic, complete response I had to chemotherapy, I am not *free of cancer*. I can't seem to rid myself of the doubts, thoughts, and fears that cancer embedded in my life. This is not to say that I spend every waking moment plagued by those thoughts; it is to acknowledge that cancer has changed the way I respond to stimuli.

Which brings me to something else—how I respond to the casual, "How are you?" greeting. I can't get myself to say I'm good. Because that's a lie. When I respond with a nonchalant, "I'm OK," it alarms most people. I think it comes off as if I'm suicidal. But OK is the new good. If I'm doing OK, it means I've had an uneventful day of not worrying about a twitch in my left eye. I sometimes try to put my best face forward and say, "I'm well."

I do wonder if other survivors put that much gravity on a simple how are you.

I have noticed another trend with survivors. Most survivors make lifestyle changes. I know a woman who has become vegan, and another who is vegetarian post-cancer. I have heard of women giving up dairy, and anything that mimics estrogen in the body such as edamame. An Indian survivor friend said she stopped using store-bought turmeric. Turmeric is an Indian staple. She now buys whole turmeric root from a local grocery store and extracts it from the root. Another woman, bless her heart, has stopped using the microwave altogether.

This is what disease does to you. When comments like, "But you're fine now," are made, I want to tell people that *there is no fine*. There is the before—and the after. What some, if not most, of us are living with is some form of trauma. A trauma great enough that we change our eating habits, stop using a microwave, and give up certain foods.

I, too, joined the bandwagon and made a small change to my lifestyle, for which I don't have much of a justification. My friend in Houston who was undergoing treatment in early 2020 pointed out that our drinking water system is contaminated and urged me to read the water report for my county. I pulled it up. As it turned out, I wasn't terribly pleased with arsenic and other elements found in the water. And on that whim, I asked Nuwan to get a reverse osmosis water system installed in the house for our drinking water. We now drink purified water. It makes me feel better. Is tap water the cause of cancers in young adults? I don't think so. I hope not. But it is a change we made to the house to help me feel better.

Now when I'm asked, "But you're fine now, right?" I like to say, "Yes. Yes, I have reverse osmosis water now."

4. RECONSTRUCTION

"**Out of suffering have emerged the strongest souls;
the most massive characters are seared with scars.**"
—Kahlil Gibran

This survivorship guide-in-progress would not be complete without acknowledging the reconstruction ruse.

It's an upgrade; you're getting a new set!
You'll have the chest of a twenty-two-year-old when you're sixty.
Lucky! You're going to be so perky.
Argh, I hate mine; they can have mine.

This is how some women and cancer survivors reacted when I shared that I was opting for a double mastectomy. I feel it was their way of expressing support: look at the brighter side; you'll get an upgrade! And for a fleeting moment, I let myself believe this would be the case for me.

A cousin who is also a surgeon said to Nuwan, "These days, reconstruction is so good, you cannot tell the difference." How I wish this were the case for me, but it couldn't be farther from the truth.

I wish a fellow survivor—or the surgeons I consulted with—had prepared me for what would be next. I hold myself accountable as well. I should have done more research; I should have asked for a second opinion. But I was consumed with fighting for my life, and the reconstruction was, after all, *just* plastic surgery. It was a means to an end, not my primary concern.

Other than chemotherapy and battling with symptoms, I struggled with my baldness. The person in the mirror looked like an old, bloated, moonfaced white guy. Yes, white; I went so pale during treatment that even my friend Randall commented on how it took him by surprise. My skin lost its color.

None of that, however, deterred my desire to be present for my children. I attended their little preschool graduations, while I was mentally prepping for the removal of my breasts. But in all this turmoil, I just did not have the bandwidth or capacity to research reconstruction.

For starters, reconstruction is not a one-time procedure; it almost always involves multiple surgeries. In my naïve, non-medical background, I thought the plastic surgeon just puts implants where breast tissue used to be, and voilà, we have breasts again—one surgery and done! Phrases like "immediate reconstruction" further confirmed my misconception. It is immediate, after all. The reality is what I call the "build a boob workshop" in which the plastic surgeon creates breasts from scratch during a lengthy surgery. I wish someone had told me how laborious reconstruction would be. The plastic surgeon uses what's at his disposal—your tissue and fat, combined with implants, to create a semblance of breasts. I call it a *semblance*, because the cold, hard truth is that the reconstructed breast will never feel the same—with an emphasis on feel. I lost all sensation to my chest wall. It hadn't occurred to me that I would not be able to feel my own breasts. Why wasn't I warned about this? The only feeling I have in my chest is this tugging sensation every time I do something that requires the participation of my pectoral muscles.

Some women have the option of using their own tissue, either from the abdomen or from the posterior. While it might sound like a win-win—get rid of fat, and use your own tissue to create the breasts—this is a major surgery. The operation can last anywhere from eight to ten hours (longer even), it involves a two-to-three-day hospital stay, and you're sent home with multiple drains. I have heard from survivors, though, that if you go this route, the aesthetic outcome and feeling of the breast is close to natural.

The length of the surgery and prolonged recovery deterred me from taking the reconstruction route. I picked the next best thing: implants.

During my double mastectomy, tissue expanders were surgically placed behind my pectoral muscles to start making room for the implants. Initially, my plastic surgeon told me that the expansion process would take six to eight weeks, followed by the implant surgery. I jotted that down for my timeline. I figured that by the time I finished radiation, I would be at the eight-week mark and could get my implants.

A first heads-up I would give to any breast cancer patient is that expanders are these barbaric devices that feel like a bulldozer trying to create space in your chest. It was painful, and the pain didn't subside. I just got used to bearing it.

I was ready to get the expanders out in the two-month time frame, as I had initially planned. However, during one of my consults with the plastic surgeon, he casually told me we would have to wait six months after my last radiation session for implant surgery. Radiation itself would be two months long, so this pushed my timeline out by eight months!

I had made a goal based on the treatment information I was privy to; the goal was to finish treatment by the end of 2018 and start a new year with cancer behind me—including all surgeries to put me back together again. *So, 2018 can burn, and I will start the new year 2019 with all of this behind me*, I thought. When my surgeon nonchalantly blew that timeline out of the water, I felt jilted. He knew I was scheduled for radiation; my radiation oncologist had even consulted with him about the tissue expanders. Radiation was not a new addition to my treatment plan. Why wasn't I given an accurate timeline?

But I quickly moved past that shock and hunkered down for physical therapy to get my arms above my head so I could start radiation. The double mastectomy had impaired my ability to move my arms. The following two months were comprised of hospital runs on Mondays through Fridays for my twenty-eight radiation sessions. Radiation was exhausting and debilitating enough for me to take disability leave from work. I still tried to be a good mother and be present for my children, while I took many naps throughout the day.

I hated how my chest looked, with the two horizontal scars across where my nipples had once been. I had inquired about nipple reconstruction. I did not want a nipple-sparing mastectomy, because I wanted no part of the cancerous breast still on me. The surgeon told me he could reconstruct a nipple using my own skin, which I could then get tattooed to match the coloring of a natural nipple. I deemed that would be the best path for me—anything to distract from the horizontal scars. The nipples would hide most of the scarring.

Halfway through radiation, I was told nipple reconstruction was not an option on the irradiated side, because the skin tends to flatten out. Again, my radiation was a known part of the treatment, so I should have been told outright that nipple reconstruction wasn't an option. When I found this out, I was upset. My nipples were already medical waste, and now I could not reconstruct them either.

I called my cousin, Vikrant, on the West Coast to voice my grievance. "I should've been told about my options up front. I'm certain that I would not have opted for a nipple sparing mastectomy. But it would've been my choice."

Vikrant was empathetic, but he reminded me, "No way would you want any part of that in your body. You have made the right decision given your age—double mastectomy, forget the nipples."

The conversation made me feel better about my decision. But the thing about being a cancer patient is that there are so many decisions out of your hands, such as the treatment plan—and decisions about what body parts you get to keep. Taking away my choice on nipples, when I had explicitly told the plastic surgeon in my first appointment with him that I wanted nipple reconstruction, was plain insensitive.

Then came the scars. I did not know that the scarring is a function of how the plastic surgeon does his work. Some use a horizontal cut, others a vertical. The thing with vertical scarring is that it elongates the breast as opposed to cutting it in half visually. Do you think I looked up the types of incisions when I made reconstruction choices? I just wanted to get through the toxic chemo and get ready for surgery.

There is so much I would have done differently. And it all starts with getting a second opinion.

Now I know that in any major, health-related situation, one must seek a second opinion. It isn't so much to counter what the first physician tells you, but more so to reaffirm that you are choosing the best path forward for yourself.

And I had a second opinion alright; I had the mother of second opinions. My company sponsors a program called Advanced Medical, through which I got a second opinion on my treatment plan from a team of reputed doctors from Harvard Medical School and Massachusetts General Hospital. You know what the second opinion didn't include? Reconstruction. Because let's face it, you have to survive the cancer first; aesthetics can be tackled later. And I completely agree with that order. At the time of treatment, I was in battle-mode. I had no physical or mental capacity to process reconstruction. I just wanted the process over with.

Here's what I discovered with the end of treatment: radiation tanning fades away and hair grows back, but you're left with scars and reconstruction outcomes. I don't consider them my battle scars or my badge of honor. I hadn't enlisted; I wasn't defending my country or my honor. These are scars that remind me of cancer. That's why I loathe them. While they show that I have endured treatment, they still remind me of what was supposed to be in their place.

•••

It is fair to question why I go into so much detail about reconstruction. As much as I hope this serves other cancer patients, I also want to highlight the privilege I feel for even having this conversation. Reconstruction isn't offered to everyone. Note how I said offered. There are countries and regions where breast reconstruction is not available, due to lack of resources or trained surgeons. And that is sad, for lack of a better word. But in places like India and the old world—sometimes even with the resources and accessibility—reconstruction is not offered.

I'll share two such instances. A next-door neighbor we knew for years growing up in Mumbai was diagnosed with breast cancer. She is a short, beautiful, Punjabi auntie with thick, long hair. She had a single mastectomy. Her male surgeon did not talk to her about implants or breast reconstruction. Instead, he told her about the special bras she could wear.

When I heard about this many years ago in my pre-cancer life, I wondered two things: Does auntie know she can opt for a double mastectomy? And why didn't the surgeon talk to her about plastic surgery? I didn't have words like "reconstruction" in my vocabulary. But I had read about celebrities getting implants after a mastectomy, and in their low-cut cleavage shots, everything appeared normal.

I only wondered this to myself. I didn't vocalize these questions.

Fast forward a decade; this time, it was in the family. My aunt was given the same dreadful diagnosis. I was older and a bit more savvy than I had been when my neighbor was ill—yet I still hadn't gone through cancer myself.

I said to my cousin, "Have you discussed the available options for plastic surgery?"

"Um, that would be rather awkward to discuss with my mother," he replied.

"Did the surgeon mention anything to her?" I asked.

"No," he answered.

I wondered if the surgeon had dismissed reconstruction for an older woman. I say older with sarcasm; my aunt was only fifty-five. Regardless of her age, this was not the surgeon's call. The surgeon's job should have been to discuss all viable options.

I realize now that breast reconstruction is a function of many factors—

including the person's health, frailty from chemotherapy, preexisting conditions, or cancer type. For example, only recently did I learn that most women with inflammatory breast cancer cannot go for immediate reconstruction. There is much I need to learn. But the point remains the same: reconstruction should be discussed.

I missed the opportunity to advocate for my aunt. I wish I had asked her about aesthetics. But I failed her. I had been in the United States for so long that I held myself culpable for losing touch with my roots. Indian families don't want to talk about breasts at the dinner table—or on the phone. I deferred to my cousin's judgment and didn't champion this conversation.

So much has changed since that event. Cancer happened to me, and with my double mastectomy, I was certain about one thing—I did not want to go flat. And I didn't want to wear prosthetic bras for the rest of my life. When I was making my decisions about plastic surgery, albeit uninformed decisions, I still had options ahead of me. In the incidences with my aunt and neighbor, those women weren't afforded the luxury.

Another reason I talk openly about this process is because the words breast reconstruction, implants, nipple sparing, and nipple tattoo are awkward to say out loud. But there, I said them. If at any point you find yourself feeling awkward about this chapter, think about how difficult it is for women to wake up with scars in place of their breasts. Suddenly, they have no nipples, and are flat chested. *That* is difficult, traumatic . . . psychologically distressing. Our role as caregivers is to advocate for our loved ones throughout this battle. I learned this after being an advocate for myself during treatment. I know how important it is to ask questions, report symptoms, seek a second opinion, and talk about aesthetic results.

I am determined not to repeat my missed advocacy opportunities again, to the best of my ability. I registered myself on a couple of cancer forums online. On one of those forums, I came across a call for participation in a video project to showcase reconstruction in minorities. What got to me was the succinct but powerful message they included. It said:

Are you a Black, Latina, or Asian woman who has recently undergone breast reconstruction? We want to hear your story. Black, Latina, and Asian women undergo breast reconstruction at half the rate of all women who have mastectomies. There are also important disparities in information delivery and visual representation of minority women in clinical imagery of breast reconstruction outcomes. For these and other reasons, there are important differences in the breast reconstruction experience among minority women that we want to explore in an upcoming video project.

Reading this echoed many aspects of my reconstruction experience and confirmed my hunch: *minority women undergo reconstruction at half the rate*. I e-mailed the team, and within a few days, I heard back. I was interviewed by a team of three by video. More than an interview, it was a conversation. Adam, Sean, and Linda were attentive, sympathetic, and shared my disappointment when they learned about the times I was misled. I also talked about my first plastic surgery consultation and the pictures that the medical team had shown me. The women in the photographs were all white.

Seeing women of color in the examples of plastic surgery done well would've abated my doubts about body image. Something that small can have a profound impact on validation.

I talked to the team about investigating greater representation, and I wondered if plastic surgeons in bigger cities used a more comprehensive racial portfolio. The video call lasted just under two hours. Towards the end, when we were getting ready to say our thank-yous and goodbyes, Sean said, "You are good storyteller!" That made me smile. I get the storytelling gene from my mother. She is a masterclass storyteller, and over the years, I picked up tricks of the trade from her.

Following the interview, I heard back from their production team, stating that they wanted to feature my story. I was one of four women selected. With the current pandemic (more on that coming up), the story would have to be recorded virtually. The FreshFly production team sent a one-man army to turn a corner of our home into a set for the next virtual interview. Nuwan and I set up an area in the basement for the crew, cleared up a corner in the living room, and tried our best to make areas aesthetically pleasing for the video shoot. The morning of the interview, when sound engineer John came over with all the equipment, he video-conferenced with Sean and Charles of FreshFly. The area of the home they picked for the interview was not one we had imagined, which just shows how little we know about videography and how talented cinematographers are. The chosen location was at the edge of our kitchen with the background of the living room, cathedral ceilings, and bay windows. It gave depth to what was otherwise a static camera angle.

John set up the tripod, boom microphone, and soft light. And then he pulled out the clapperboard! It was a production, alright, once the clapperboard entered the scene. He wrote my name and scene 1, take 1. This is really happening!

Before the start of shooting, Sean said, "Marker," and John said, "Niyati, scene 1, take 1," and clapped the board. At the end of each session, Sean would say, "Tail slate," and John would clap the board upside down, and that would stop the clock timer.

Being engineers, and curious as we are, Nuwan asked, "I'm guessing the slate makes the editor's job a bit easier…?" That's when John interjected and said it was also used to synchronize picture and sound with the help of the clap. To the celebrities who are reading this, thinking, *what's the big deal?* It was for me! It was my first official production. Let's just say that I was high on life that afternoon doing the interview, and it all culminated with a terrible headache from the stress of it. Ha.

If you've read my first book, you will know by now that I'm a professional thanksgiver. Prolific note writing, sending thank-you e-mails, and the occasional bowtie or scarf as a token of my appreciation is my way of expressing gratitude. I sent one such thank-you e-mail to the FreshFly team, and this is a snippet of the response I got from director Sean.

Niyati,

Thank YOU for your courage in sharing your story, generosity in sharing your life, and hospitality in opening your home (literally and virtually) [to] us.

We consider it an honor to be entrusted with crafting your story to share with the world, and we promise to do so as thoughtfully and artfully as possibly.

I read this e-mail out to my sister as I tried to get my head around the humility and gratitude expressed by the FreshFly team. They were thanking me for sharing *my* story and applauding *my courage*. I felt like I was in a parallel universe; an accomplished production team was thanking me.

Priya said simply, "That is how it should be."

Back home, it is harder to have experiences like these; the sheer numbers in India leave little time or energy for empathy. But really, each story should be treated with the respect it deserves—as mine was that day.

Something else happened when I posted my information on the cancer forum. Two women of Indian descent private messaged me to learn from my experience. One lives in Illinois, and the other in Massachusetts. I talked them through the options I was aware of and the path I chose, and even video-chatted with them individually. One of the ladies, let's call her Asha, was thinking about going flat. Since I don't know what that's like, I reached out to my network. My cancer survivor friend, Beth, got me in touch with her friend, who chose to go flat after a mastectomy. She said she would be happy to talk to Asha. I put the two women in touch, and took a step back. Asha later told me she had the most inspirational talk with Beth's friend and felt more certain than ever that she wanted to go flat, too. Good for Asha!

I am hopeful that being on forums like this affords me greater opportunities to mentor survivor sisters. Even if I can't directly help, I am confident in my growing network; I know I can find someone with that experience. If anybody's pain and uncertainty can be diminished from my experience, I call it a good day to be alive.

5. HAVE FAITH

> "No one is without troubles, without personal hardships and genuine challenges. That fact may not be obvious, because most people don't advertise their woes and heartaches. But nobody, not even the purest heart, escapes life without suffering battle scars."
> —Richelle E. Goodrich

There is an inextricable tie between human hardship and a higher being. When we can't make sense of situations, we may rely on our predetermined religion (predetermined by our birth and our parents' choices) or find a source of hope that speaks to us. Even the pseudo-religious turn to mainstream prayer and chanting to invoke divine intervention.

Long before cancer changed my narrative, I started to learn how faith can be misused, and in small ways, I took a stance. Here's how it started. Many moons ago, a dear friend of mine, Kelsey, was pregnant with her first child. We celebrated the twelve-week, "out-of-danger" mark, as she told me, "The second trimester is meant to be glorious."

However, things did not progress as we had wished, and Kelsey suffered a miscarriage. I was young and stupid, and I asked an ignorant question.

"Are you sure? How do you know you miscarried?" I assumed it was a bit of blood loss she was nervous about, when in all honesty, I thought, the baby is fine.

Kelsey said, stone cold, "I saw the fetus in the toilet bowl."

If that description is not visceral enough, I don't know what is. I felt so stupid asking her how she knew. My heart broke for my dear friend. She cried bitterly, while a childless, unmarried, unqualified me tried to console her. I wanted to take away her pain, but I had no words of wisdom. I couldn't do much more than lend my shoulder to cry on.

In subsequent weeks, Kelsey told me about how people around her tried to make her feel better by saying things like, "This baby wasn't part of God's plan," or, "God loved the baby so much that He couldn't part with it." Some suggested that Kelsey "now had an angel in heaven looking down on her." Some urged her to "have faith, you can try again."

This reasoning infuriated me and often left Kelsey in tears, feeling worse than she already did. The statements about God's plan baffled me. It's ironic that a decade later, I would be fed the same "God's plan" explanation. For Kelsey, I wondered: What was God's plan after all? To give Kelsey an opportunity to hear the heartbeat of her baby, fall in love instantly, and then take it away?

Comments around "just have faith" are insulting to the sufferer. Kelsey had faith; she had all the faith in the world. She is a devout Christian, God-fearing churchgoer, and pious woman. Saying "have faith" implies that her faith was somehow lacking the first time around, and *if she only had enough faith*, the next time would deliver results.

Some said, "It wasn't meant to be." I struggled to get my head around the uselessness of that statement. Obviously, it wasn't meant to be; she lost the baby. And to the wise men and women who told Kelsey, "Everything happens for a reason," I want to ask what is the reason? Seriously, tell me the reason. Please spell it out for me. I'm going to preempt this though—we mothers don't need a miscarriage or two to love our live-born babies. I don't accept a reason of, "Having lost a child, you will be all the more grateful once you deliver a healthy baby."

I believe the root cause of these faith statements is that we are uncomfortable with people's pain. We scramble to minimize it, offer up idealistic future scenarios, or rummage through our bag of clichés to pull out something insensitive like, "It was probably for the best."

Kelsey lacked the ability to be mad at people. Instead, she internalized their comments, and in moments of weakness, she would confide in me.

I looked my beautiful, blond-haired, blue-eyed friend in her eyes and said, "If anyone says you can try again, mention that it is not a pair of jeans that you can replace. It is a baby, your baby inside you, that has died. When loved ones talk about trying again, it might be because they can't deal with the present loss, so they want to dream up a future baby and proclaim that once you have your baby, you will forget all about the miscarriage."

Kelsey struggled with a range of emotions. She felt like her body had failed her. She started looking for reasons why this had happened to her—everything that she might have done wrong—even "risky" behavior like drinking coffee. She really does live on the edge, that party animal with her one coffee a day!

Kelsey reasoned with me, "It must've been the morning coffee, Niyati."

I talked her off the ledge; it wasn't the coffee.

Kelsey also had a few statisticians pretending to be her friends who reminded her about how common miscarriages are, because what better way to deal with trauma than to normalize it with numbers. Even I knew better than that, and I'm a numbers girl, math enthusiast, and spreadsheet guru. To me, citing pregnancy loss numbers is like me telling you, "One hundred percent of human beings will experience death in their lifetime." Useful, right?

In one of our conversations, Kelsey pointed out to me, "Niyati, the report stated that it was a spontaneous abortion." I was gutted at the cruelty of that medical terminology. She then asked me something profound, "Why did this happen to me?"

I told her "I don't know."

I was honest; I didn't know why this had happened to her. I didn't offer up godly reasons, or talk about angels in heaven. I never once talked about trying again. That would have been plain cruel.

After the miscarriage, Kelsey struggled to conceive again. Two years ticked by, and unsolicited advice came in the form of adoption: "You can always adopt. I've heard of a couple that adopted and then got pregnant."

Adoption is not the stepping-stone to the real prize of having that biological child you wanted. Adoption is the prize! It is a miracle in my mind when a lucky family with love to give and a child with endless potential find each other.

I told Kelsey to do what was right for her. If she wanted to keep trying, she should. If she wanted to do IVF, she should. If she wanted to adopt, she should.

She wanted a break. She deserved it.

In subsequent years, she gave birth to a boy and a girl, and in between the two, she suffered two miscarriages. We went through the gamut on repeat. Only this time, the comments were even more callous, if that were possible. Friends reminded her of how lucky she was. "At least you have your boy; you're lucky you can still get pregnant."

Fast forward eight some years, and I'm getting schooled on God's plan. I feel if there's one thing cancer patients have in common with couples struggling to carry a successful pregnancy to term, it is desperation. I don't know the struggles of conceiving; what I do have is empathy. When I was diagnosed and an ignoramus said to me, "God only gives you what you can handle" and later I heard another echo, "God doesn't give you anything you can't handle," I wanted to scream. How does God play into this narrative?

I admit, I don't know the origin of this verse or the context in which it was written. But God's plan to rationalize someone's suffering is unwarranted. The way I interpret it, when you say that to someone diagnosed with cancer, it implies: God thinks you can handle cancer, so he has chosen this path for you. Conversely if you are weak and cannot handle cancer, then it won't happen to you.

That makes no sense at all. And frankly speaking, it does harm to my faith to think of God in those terms. I don't believe that I am being punished or tested for being strong.

I am in touch with cancer survivors who have a renewed trust in the Almighty. And some say with gratitude, "it was part of God's plan," and how "blessed they are for knowing God is with them." There are survivors who talk about "how much brighter and more wonderful life is now." I'm happy for them and their discovery. But for me: my world was bright and wonderful before cancer. I didn't need the disease to help me appreciate rainbows and sunshine. I am not in that group of born-again spirituals.

Not for a moment am I grateful I got this disease.

There are several things I *am* grateful for: my family, the cancer care I received, and arriving at the pathologic complete response (PCR) after chemotherapy. I am grateful to be in remission—and thankful that we had children before I was diagnosed.

But never once have I thought it was God's plan for me to get this disease. My faith in God is unwavering, and I refuse to believe He would have planned such suffering for me, at a time when two tiny humans depended on me.

I know a survivor who lost her trust in the Almighty post-diagnosis. Her story is tough; I sympathize with her. She was diagnosed with hormone positive breast cancer, and she has the BRCA gene mutation. As a result, she has been asked to take medication for ovarian suppression for the next ten years. She is in her thirties, doesn't have children, and is single. We spoke a few times over coffee, and she walked me through her thought process. Her options were either to remove her ovaries or do this chemical ovarian suppression with the hope that after ten years, she can try to conceive. She said to me, with resignation in her voice, "By the time this is all said and done, I will be forty-five and wanting to get pregnant with ovaries that hopefully wake up after ten years of chemical suppression and provide viable eggs." When she talked about her faith, I listened, provided support free of judgement, and did not try to baptize or convert her. It was not my place to brush off her sorrow and offer up *God's plan*. I reverted to what I told Kelsey with her miscarriages, "I don't know why this happened to you. I am sorry."

Suffering and hardship occur in everyone's life. As human beings, we search for the truth—a reason behind why things happen, and how. It's as if finding that reason will somehow protect us from future harm. But disease does not play by the rules. And sometimes, regardless of your religion, spirituality, faith in a higher being, or firm atheism, you get dealt a bad hand. In that situation, I give you permission to accept not knowing why your friend, colleague, or neighbor had that miscarriage, got that cancer—insert any human suffering into this statement.

I would hold off on revealing God's plan; leave that up to Him.

So, what is my grand plan for reconciling why disease, tragedy, and loss happen? I don't have one. I don't know the whys behind human suffering. And I am OK with not knowing.

6. PARITY

"For mad I may be, but I will never be convenient."
—Jennifer Donnelly, Revolution

At this point in the book, you might get a sense of what makes me tick. So there should be no surprises when I tell you that gender-based discrimination is the bane of my existence. I cannot stand to witness discrimination against women and have ample experience in the subject. I am drawn to women's rights and feel a heightened sense of apprehension when I see my kind being treated unfairly. I feel it is my duty to alleviate the suffering of women in any way I can.

An issue dear to my heart is the treatment of widows in Indian society—or any society where widows are treated as second-class. There is a chapter in my first book called "Fire in my soul" where I talk about how society treated my mother, my sister, and me after my father was killed in a car crash. *To think someday I would put "there is a chapter in my first book" in a sentence, while writing my second book, is an exercise in stupefaction.* When some of my childhood friends read the book, they were shocked that my mother, Priya, and I were subjected to such unfair and unwarranted treatment. In that book, I addressed the ugliness of being a widow, how society looks at it as a curse, and how a family without a father or brother—no man of the house—is seen as a lesser unit. An old friend from home, Aysha, called me after she read my book. She was apologetic and on the verge of tears. Aysha had no idea of the atrocities we had faced. In her defense, we were all children. I didn't expect Aysha to know or comprehend that while the entirety of the apartment complex was invited to the Mehta wedding during my childhood, our names were left off the guest list because having a widow at a wedding is considered a bad omen. Aysha asked me if her parents took any part in mistreating my mother. Of course, they did not. Aysha's reaction and apology on behalf of what was done to us made it clear that she was not raised with that mindset.

With *Unafraid*, I opened the doors to the "dead dads club" by sharing my experience candidly. Women who lost their fathers early in life opened up to me and shared their stories. The commonality of the ill treatment is appalling. While I feel what my mother suffered was unjustifiable, some anecdotes I heard from the deep South were much worse. Widows shunned by their own family, or a widowed mother not allowed to give her daughter's hand away in marriage. This has got to change. And it is already, with my generation of strong, independent women who will no longer put up with inequality or stand by to watch our mothers being mistreated.

Priya had our mother stand in her wedding and perform wedding rites. She made it clear to my mother that there is no giving away of her hand in marriage. In Hindu ceremonies, this ritual is called *kanya daan; kanya* is daughter and *daan* is donation. The girl's parents donate their daughter in the wedding. Suffice it to say, there isn't an equivalent *putra daan*; sons are not up for donation.

I followed Priya's example: my mother performed wedding rituals and didn't have *kanya daan*. When the priest blessed me with a *shloka* (prayer) that went like this, "And may God bless you with a thousand sons," I interrupted and asked him to repeat the *shloka* with, "May God bless you with a thousand daughters."

∙∙∙

By now, something else you must have concluded about me is that if there's a taboo topic, I will likely find a public forum to talk about it—or worse still, write a book on it.

Today's taboo topic is *periods*. Just as I learned the stigma associated with cancer spans across cultures, the taboo and secrecy around menstruation is not unique to India. Across the developing world, women deal with their periods in inconceivable ways. Illiteracy and poverty further mystify menstruation.

Before I get started, I need to come clean with you. I was in my thirties when I finally gained a positive association with periods. After breastfeeding my son for two hard years, my periods returned. I was inexplicably ashamed; I felt the sadness I used to feel as a teenager. I talked to my obstetrician about my misguided sorrow.

"Degaulle, I cannot explain it, but I am feeling sad. My periods are back."

He simply said, "Niyati, this means you're fertile." That right there, a simple statement, shed a positive light on periods. I am embarrassed that at the age of thirty-three, a physician had to link periods and fertility for me, as if it was a revelation. It's not that I didn't know how my body worked or about the birds and the bees; I was just not used to thinking about my body's process that way.

Growing up in India, getting periods meant entering a secret pact, and there were strict instructions to *never talk about getting your period*. The disposal of sanitary products was like trying to rid oneself of incriminating evidence. You were on secret-ops; leave no trace, and don't get caught. For me, along with many girls my age, entering puberty was a nightmare. It's like no one gave me a heads-up on this; I was just flung into adolescence.

Staining my white school uniform skirt was a constant cause of stress during those few days of the month. I still remember, if your skirt got stained, you would have to go to one of the nuns, Sister Mercedes, and ask for a replacement skirt. It was so embarrassing, and Sister Mercedes never had a kind word to share. She would make some snide comment, then act like it was the biggest inconvenience for her to find a skirt of the right size, then follow the hand-off by a blunt warning: "Don't stain this one. Bring back the skirt, clean and ironed." I remember thinking to myself, *why aren't these nuns like Fraulein Maria from* The Sound of Music?

On more than one occasion, I asked my mother if I could just stay home for a few days. Taking a concealed sanitary napkin to school and then extracting said item without your classmates seeing it was such a daunting task, and if anyone found out, I would be mortified. But my mother always told us that "all women go through this," and we "mustn't let anything affect our education, least of all a natural phenomenon."

But every month, I felt like I was carrying this shameful burden.

I had another brush with period-indignity around the age of fifteen. A few of us girls were visiting a famous temple in Mumbai dedicated to Lord Ganesha, called Siddhivinayak Temple. One of my friends, let's call her Meena, walked with us to the doorstep but did not enter the temple. She said she was unwell. I found that odd, since she didn't appear to be outwardly ill. When I got home, I told my mother about Meena's odd behavior and how the others seemed to understand the situation. What am I missing? My mother told me that Meena was likely on her period, and that it was common practice for women to refrain from praying then, because a woman is considered impure during her period.

I'm sorry, what? There's a time when I am less holy?

I asked my mother, "Why would God have a gripe against the very body he created? The time of the month doesn't alter my desire to pray or taint my soul."

Moreover, I argued to myself, how was this anybody's business?

My mother's answer left a lasting impression on my young mind: "You eat when you're on your period; you sleep when you're on your period; you to go to school, do your homework, and play with your friends. Why would you not pray when you're on your period?" These were archaic traditions that were not observed in my home. Clearly, she shared my mindset that the tradition was absurd.

As I became more comfortable in my own skin, I wanted to learn more about the taboo surrounding periods. I read articles about the origins behind menstrual customs and talked to Indian friends about what they had learned as kids. A friend told me that when his mother was on her period, she wasn't allowed in the kitchen. A girlfriend told me she was forbidden from feeding her toddler son during her time of the month. Yet she was expected to go to work—strong enough to earn a living, but too unsanitary to touch her own child, who by the way is only here because this woman, my friend, had her periods and was fertile.

Menstrual practices in India have a deep-rooted history. Some say that periods make a woman weak, and she needs the rest. Hindu theologians cite Vedic literature and claim that menstruation causes an imbalance in the universe, and during that time women have negative energy. Whatever the justification, it is a tool to restrict women's freedom and shame them. While we can debate over why these customs were put in place or the value of preserving tradition, the plight of women is forgotten.

There are period huts, literally huts, where young girls are banished to spend the nights during their unholy time. The promoters of period huts describe them as a safe nook for women to recuperate. But period huts exist in the murky corners of wicked opportunistic minds. Girls often get raped in period huts, and hence are terrified at being forced to spend the night away from family. Period huts are a convenient arrangement for pedophiles—and well, rapists.

Other than the safety aspect—even though no sentence should start with "other than safety"—there is a direct impact to girls' education when they don't have access to menstrual products, waste management, and the privacy of a toilet. This lack of access to necessary resources is called period poverty, which has long-term consequences on literacy and a girl's future. Around the world, two out of three girls avoid school because of the shame around menstruation and the lack of access. Heck, even I asked my mother if I could stay home from school; imagine those who don't have access to the products they need.

Telling your pubescent daughter to hide her sanitary napkins strips her of her dignity. Banishing a mother from the kitchen teaches boys that there's something unclean about their mother—and women in general. We must get rid of these notions at the family level. Destigmatizing periods, educating boys and girls about how the body changes, and teaching girls how to use sanitary products are a start.

Something else that can help influence mindsets for the better is legislation. One such recent example of triumph happened in southern India. Sabrimala Temple in the state of Kerala is a shrine for the celibate god, Ayyappa. As a pilgrimage site for Hindus, each year the temple sees close to fifty million devotees. The pilgrims are mostly men, because women between the ages of ten and fifty—those of reproductive age—are banned from entering the temple. The argument from temple leadership is that such women could distract the deity Ayyappa from his avowed celibacy and entice him.

That's not all. The pilgrimage to Sabrimala involves a purification ritual.

One is supposed to refrain from meat, alcohol, and sex for forty-one days before paying respects to Ayyappa. Part of this forty-one-day fast also stipulates no contact with menstruating women—you know, because we are impure and all. Let the damnation continue.

This takes menstrual humiliation to the next level. I thought it was preposterous to inquire if a girl is on her period before going to a temple, but banning women completely is batshit crazy. OK, not a complete ban: the "old hags" of fifty and above are permitted to worship. That is a slap in the face for menopausal women. What does this say about how our culture thinks of postmenopausal women? This is not a rhetorical question, because I'll spell it out: after the age of fifty, even God won't find you attractive. The thing is, we menstruating, childbearing, breastfeeding, postmenopausal women go to work, do chores, care for our families, and volunteer in the community. We are not impure, weak, unsanitary, or overly tantalizing—at any age or any time of the month. Placing the burden of a deity's celibacy on women is a derogatory notion, as it paints a woman as a temptress, femme fatale, and provocateur.

Oppression of women in any society can be overturned—made illegal or punishable by putting laws in place. This isn't the complete answer, but it starts to influence mindsets. If laws are enacted, we can eventually change people's mentality.

In 2018, the Supreme Court of India did just that, citing religious patriarchy—a notion that other world religions share to varying degrees—and lifting the ban on women in the Sabrimala temple. While right-wing Hindus opposed the ruling, it was the ruling nonetheless, and has been accepted. I call it a "one small step for women, one giant leap for humanity" moment. I hope this precedent carries over to everyday family life. If the Sabrimala Temple lifted its ban on women, why must we banish our mothers and sisters from temples?

Continuing my ode and debt to my family, I want to share that my father did not restrict my mother in any way, when it came to her freedom, hygiene, or piety during any day of the month. It seems ludicrous that I'm even stating this. My mother taught my sister and me about feminine hygiene and never once used words such as impure or weak. I went to temple on my periods, and I prayed with a pure heart. With this body God gave me, I bore two children.

•••

In any given country, there is room for improvement in women's equality that can be made by amending laws. A small but significant thing we could do here in the United States is to provide tax-free menstruation products. Thirty-five out of fifty states have a tampon tax, sometimes known as a "pink tax." But all fifty states offer a tax-exempt price tag for erectile dysfunction medicine, because it is considered medically necessary. Let me spell that out: Viagra is tax-free. When I learned this, I had an epic face-palm moment. Out of curiosity, I checked my state's laws; Indiana taxes menstrual products. But as I write this book and talk about no taxation on menstruation, the world is taking steps towards eradicating period poverty. Scotland is the first country in the world to provide feminine hygiene products not just as tax-exempt—but completely free. Way to set an example, Scotland! These initiatives will go a long way in empowering and improving the quality of life for women.

In my lifetime, there is another law that I hope gets overturned in India and wherever else it may exist. The Indian Penal Code provides an exception to the definition of rape. Unwilling sexual intercourse between a husband and wife is not considered rape. Furthermore, the law states that a wife is presumed to deliver perpetual consent to sex after entering marital relations.

Perpetual.

Let this sink in: in a country where arranged marriages are widely practiced, marital rape is not criminalized. India gets to be in the league of some three dozen countries, including Singapore, that don't offer protection to wives. I don't want India to be in this despicable league. The origins of this law date back to the mid-1850s, when India as a colony adopted British laws. But I don't use that as an excuse, because England has since moved on. And outdated laws should be rewritten. I strongly believe that if India as a nation, the largest democracy in the world, wants to systematically eradicate the rape culture we are tainted with, we need to start here: criminalize nonconsensual sex regardless of marital status.

There is more where this comes from. Let me look at India's neighbors, for instance. In Pakistan, there is a wife-beating bill supported by the Council of Islamic Ideology. It states that a man can "lightly beat" his wife as a form of discipline if she does one of the following: defies his commands, does not dress up per her husband's desires, refuses intercourse, or does not bathe after intercourse or when she is on her periods. If someone could just define *light beating* to me . . . OK, this is not to say all Pakistani husbands are beating their wives. It is not to assume that people even follow this nonsense of not dressing as per a husband's code. It is only to remind you that if such defiance occurs, the wife has no legal protection. It is not to demonize all males of that or any society; it is to highlight areas where women don't have legal protection.

Outdated laws don't have a place in society. A lot of this comes down to legislative inertia; laws were put in place back in the stone ages, and we haven't bothered to change them. Yes, changing the law is cumbersome, but it needs to be done.

When I think about one of the wealthiest, seemingly progressive Middle Eastern countries, my mind goes to the United Arab Emirates (UAE). Images of Dubai, Burj Khalifa, and Yas Marina Formula One racetrack come to mind, with the sand dunes in between. Rape law is pretty messed up there, and this is not unique to the UAE. Women who report rape in the UAE are often charged with adultery and having illicit sexual relations. Emirati law can sentence the rape victim to imprisonment, flogging, or stoning. The burden of proof is on the victim. In order to prove rape, the victim needs to procure a confession from the rapist. Has your jaw dropped to the floor? Leave it there, because it gets even more absurd. Along with this signed confession from the rapist, she needs to bring forward four male witnesses to the rape for the accusation to stick and be tried as a criminal offense.

Since UAE is a magnet for expatriates from all over the world, if assaulted, some misguided women report rape, because they assume protection from law enforcement agencies. When they can't get that darned confession and those four male witnesses, they are thrown into prison. When the women reporting sexual assault are British or American—code for white—the charges tend to get dropped due to international outcry. You read that correctly, the charges against the rape victim *for getting raped* are dropped.

The perpetrator goes free, of course.

•••

For me, gender parity follows Maslow's Hierarchy of Needs. According to Maslow, human beings have five categories of needs, starting at the base and moving towards the apex: physiological needs, safety, love, esteem, and self-actualization. Higher needs in the pyramid begin to emerge only when people feel they have sufficiently satisfied lower-level needs. When you have a roof over your head and don't have to worry about food insecurity, you can think about finding a partner and starting a family.

Similarly, to achieve gender equality, you need to pass each tier's requirements and move up.

Using Maslow's model as my guide, here's my Gender Parity Hierarchy of Needs.

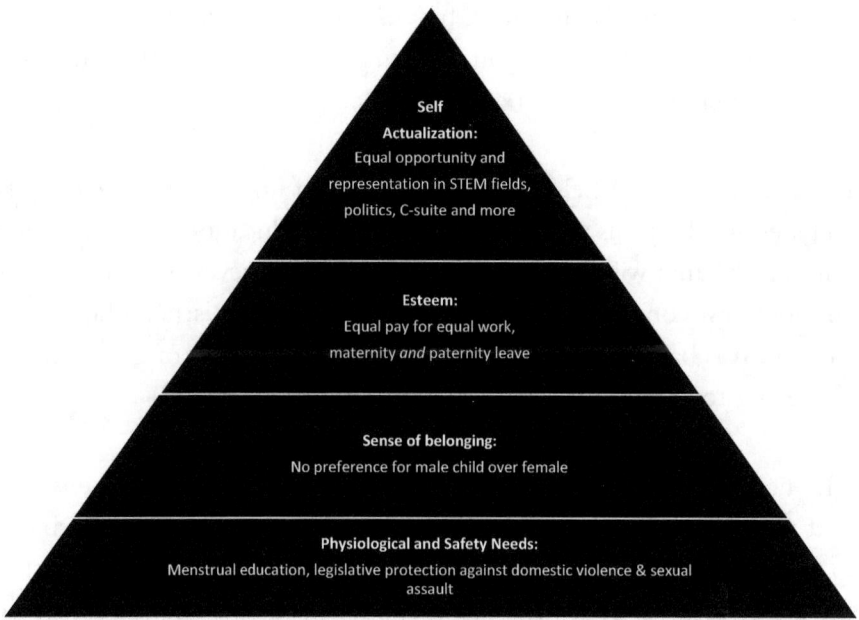

Cultures in the bottom tier of physiological and safety needs are busy dealing with menstrual education, hygiene, eradicating period poverty, and tackling sexual assault. Once they have a better handle on those lower-level needs, they can move up the pyramid to a sense of belonging.

For me, this sense of belonging starts in the womb. The strong preference of male over female children in India is the root of indiscriminate cases of female feticide. In plain English, this means aborting the female fetus. It became so rampant in India, many times against the mother's wishes but forced by the in-laws, that India has made it illegal to find out the sex of the child during pregnancy.

The preference for a boy is not unique to India. In China, when they had a one-couple one-child law, families that could afford to have a second child might try only if the first were a girl. The Chinese government in effect was telling its people: "It's not ideal that your one and only child is a girl, so go ahead and try for a second child, if you can afford it." Couples that hit the jackpot by having a boy in their first and only attempt are done. "No more babies for you." Because who would want to try for a second, when the first is that coveted male?

For me, this sense of belonging tier is the most important. We can make all types of lofty goals around gender equality, education, and leadership, but none of that will matter if that girl child was never wanted—or was considered a consolation prize. I put the onus of this need heavily on women. It is baffling and disheartening when a mother or grandmother isn't eager to welcome that girl child.

The next level up is esteem. To reach this tier, let's start with ensuring that women don't need to obtain legal permission from their husbands to work (this still exists in some countries, people!). Once we are part of the workforce, this tier demands equal pay for equal work and enjoys the perks of paid and protected maternity leave. Countries that are in the top echelon of this tier offer comparable paternity leave, leveling the playing field when it comes to raising a family.

Finally, at the apex is self-actualization, where women have equal opportunity and protection to attain their full potential. Seeing more women in STEM fields, I personally root for women in engineering, research, and medicine. When I talk about changing legislation, of course we need ethical, top-notch lawyers; but having more women in politics can drive the decisions on the urgency to change archaic laws and eliminate things like the pink tax. I would love to see more women executives in CEO, CFO, COO, and CIO positions of power and influence. That is my gender parity pipe dream.

7. STANDING ON THE SHOULDERS OF GIANTS

> "What is success?
> To laugh often and much; to win the respect of intelligent people and the affection of children; to earn the appreciation of honest critics and endure the betrayal of false friends; to appreciate the beauty; to find the best in others; to leave the world a bit better, whether by a healthy child, a garden patch Or a redeemed social condition; to know even one life has breathed easier because you have lived. This is to have succeeded!"
> —Ralph Waldo Emerson

I'm sensing I've done enough to convince you that I'm a badass. *She fought cancer, advocates for women, is a taboo terminator* . . . As much as I would like to lap up all the praise, I feel like I'm being deceitful if I don't reveal to you *who* I come from. The blood in my veins is from a strong and proud lineage. And while I share my family's story with you, I am certain it is not unique. We are descendants of the greatest generation that ever lived (that of World War II). As you indulge me in my ancestral narrative, I also urge you to think about where you came from.

Manohar Rao Koli, my maternal grandfather, was born on June 12, 1912. *Aajoba* (*Aajoba* is grandfather in Marathi) was a toddler at the onset of World War I (WWI). He grew up in India at a time when we were ruled by the British, and was a teenager during the Great Depression.

The Great Depression is often described as the worst economic downturn in the history of the industrialized world. Key phrase, industrialized world. We learned about this in history textbooks, in my convent school in Mumbai. We were taught about the U.S. stock market crash of 1929 and how cities were hit hard. We learned how the perils of the Great Depression stoked the flames of Hitler's power. We even learned about our colonizers and how the United Kingdom hadn't yet fully recovered from WWI.

It irks me now as a grown adult that we were not taught about the devastating consequences that both WWI and the Great Depression had on India and her citizens. Being a colony is never fun. Think loss of rights, slavery, use of the Indian economy and resources to fill Her Majesty's treasury, man-made famines as a tool of oppression, the infamous salt tax . . . I could go on. Being a colony when your ruler fought *the war to end all wars* followed by an economic depression of epic proportions—is downright shit . . . I mean frightfully dire.

Aajoba's parents were farmers. Their land, however, belonged to a *zamindar* (*zamindar* means landlord in Persian). The *zamindar* owed taxes to the British Raj (empire). In other words, our land wasn't ours. The existing imperialistic policies were intensified to bolster the British economy during the Great Depression, while bleeding India dry.

For Aajoba's parents, this meant that rent on their farmland skyrocketed, while the cost of produce they toiled hard for plummeted. Farmers were forced to give up any gold or silver that belonged to the family to pay their debts. I am not certain how my great grandparents managed to keep their heads above water, but I do know that Aajoba grew up with food insecurity. The next meal wasn't a guarantee.

In this environment, my great grandfather, *Aneji*, in his infinite wisdom, decided that Aajoba's education must be a priority. He could not afford to send all of his children to school, three boys and two girls, so he picked the eldest son. Aajoba attended primary school in the village. However, this was the only school, and it maxed out at fifth grade. By the time children were ten years old, they were back on the farm tilling, plowing, and doing whatever else farmers do. (Full disclosure: I know nothing about farming.) Aneji realized that Aajoba needed to go to the big city to get an education—where there were schools, colleges, and universities; where he would have a future. The "big city" closest to them was Nagpur.

Aneji wrote a letter to relatives in Nagpur asking them if he could send his son to live with them and attend school. He would of course pay school fees but needed somewhere for Aajoba to stay—room and board. One set of relatives agreed and asked him to bring Aajoba over. The father-son duo took a train to Nagpur for the drop-off. When they got to the relatives' place, the relatives had a change of heart, suddenly realizing, "We will have one more mouth to feed," and withdrew their offer to house Aajoba.

It had been a long day—a day with no meals, a train ride to Nagpur, the rejection from relatives, and no future in sight. Dejected and hungry, Aneji bought some peanuts for Aajoba to stave off the young boy's hunger. They were waiting at the train station when they ran into an old acquaintance. I don't know the name of this acquaintance, so I'm going to call him Mr. Meherbaan (*meherbaan* means kind in Hindi). Mr. Meherbaan asked my great grandfather what brought them to Nagpur. Aneji narrated the story of their misfortune. Without hesitation, Mr. Meherbaan said, "Nonsense. If your boy wants to go to school, he should go to school! Manohar can stay with my family. He can earn his keep by doing chores, running errands, and helping around the house while he attends school." And just like that, my great grandfather handed over his ten-year-old son to Mr. Meherbaan.

Being an errand boy afforded Aajoba room and board. However, he didn't have a penny to his name. He needed money to buy books, notebooks, anything—even loose sheets of paper so that he could write, take notes, practice algebra. Aajoba had seen other kids taking notes in their notebooks during class, but he went to school without one. For a few days, he tried to commit the lessons to memory, but this process was clearly not sustainable. He needed to procure paper to write stuff down.

Back in the 1920s when there were traveling shows—musical performances being held in town or in neighboring towns—they would draw big crowds. The form of advertising a hundred years ago was rudimentary—some bugger would rock up in his cycle rickshaw full of event flyers. He would throw flyers up in the air and hand them to passersby. People would read the advertisements and promptly toss the paper. The flyers were printed single-sided and that, my friends, was all the paper Aajoba needed! Aajoba collected as many tossed flyers as he could find.

Still, my grandfather had a lot of pride. Just because he could source paper didn't mean he would attend school with some loose sheets that had random artwork on one side. He wanted a notebook like his classmates. So, notebook it was; he stitched together the flyers. Aajoba made notebooks for himself with recycled paper well before his time; now that's a sustainability goal we should all be incorporating!

Education continued to take priority. As Aajoba was close to finishing high school, Aneji found a job as a tax revenue collector. This afforded the Koli family a meager but stable income.

The perk of that job was pride. Aneji traveled with the head revenue collector from district to district—by elephant! That's right, my great grandfather rode an elephant to work, traveling like an Indian king. This revenue collector job meant that Aajoba could dream about going to university. Aajoba had an aptitude for math, an intellectual capacity for engineering, and a fascination with electricity.

I am speculating here, but I have a theory behind why Aajoba was captivated by electricity. When he was a young boy, as the evening set in, the house would go dark. They had oil lamps in the house; however, the oil used for lighting a lamp was the same oil used for cooking, and they didn't have enough to do both. The priority was clear: the daily quota of oil would be used for cooking, to feed mouths. This meant their evenings and nights were spent in darkness.

Aajoba wanted to excel in academics—not just to pass some test but to have the top score. He wanted to be first in his class and was willing to put in the hard work for it. So, to study after sundown, he would take his books to the street corner where there was a streetlamp. My grandfather studied there, under its dim evening light. That is how determined he was. He felt no shame in doing what he needed to do to be the best in school. My theory is that this experience is what motivated him to study electrical engineering and ultimately work for the state electricity board, or what we in the U.S. call a utility company or power grid. I have a feeling those evenings of walking to the street corner and sitting on the ground under the glow of a streetlamp left an indelible mark on him.

Aajoba pursued a bachelor's in electrical engineering—a BEE, as they called it. The irony of this? I hold a bachelor's in electrical and computer engineering (BECE), following in his footsteps. It was Aajoba's drive and determination decades before I was born that would be a part of me, even after I had cancer, as I sought to turn my hardest days into light.

You see when I claimed I didn't do this alone? I have a lineage I need to measure up to. A lineage I *want* to measure up to.

There were only ten engineering schools in India in the 1930s. To put this in perspective, by the 1930s, the United States had three times as many universities offering a degree in engineering to a substantially smaller population. Aajoba, through his excellent test scores, secured a coveted spot in Jadavpur Engineering College, a university on the east coast of India.

Aneji's stable income made it possible for Aajoba to attend college. Aneji gave half of his monthly income to pay his son's tuition. He then managed a household, wife, two daughters, and two additional sons with the remainder of his salary.

They never had enough money for textbooks, though. So, Aajoba attended engineering classes without a single textbook to his name. But he found a way around it.

Early into his engineering degree, Aajoba made friends with a fellow student who belonged to the affluent Jhunjhunwala family in Calcutta. Their friendship rose from mutual respect. Young Jhunjhunwala and Aajoba often studied together, which meant Aajoba had access to a textbook, his friend's textbook. Feel free to assume here that Jhunjhunwala was a male friend; I don't think there were female engineering students at Aajoba's university back then. My grandfather, being who he is, took it one step further. He asked permission to study from the textbooks at nights when his mate was asleep. Jhunjhunwala had no issues with the arrangement.

Time and time again, Aajoba removed obstacles and advocated for himself to get on the path to success. The result of this determination and perseverance was that he earned a gold medal for being first in his class for electrical engineering at his university.

After earning his degree, you might think that Aajoba found a job, got married, raised five daughters, and was a proud grandfather… and the rest, as they say, was history. But it wasn't so.

Searching for a job was an eye-opener for Aajoba. For starters, there weren't any jobs to be had, so he went a year with no luck landing a position. The guilt and shame got to him. Guilt that his family lived on the fringe of poverty to enable his degree. Shame that after all the hard work he couldn't find a job to support his parents and siblings.

Aajoba couldn't take it anymore and ran away from home. Not without a note, though; he promised his parents he would return when he found a job and could contribute to the family. Aajoba inquired at establishments in neighboring towns and villages, but to no avail. The job hunt eventually took him some six hundred miles north to Delhi. And there, he finally got a job in a sugar factory. The factory manager was the first to inform Aajoba that his degree was not an engineering degree—but rather a diploma, a vocational certificate. Aajoba was blindsided. How was it that he did all the courses, credit hours, and paid tuition for engineering school—but got an unrecognizable degree?

Aajoba had attended university during a time when a system of credit hours or centralized governing body did not quite exist. He didn't realize that he graduated with a diploma in engineering, but not a degree. That translated to an associate's degree in today's world. The nuances of college degrees and what they meant were beyond his parents' ken. Worse yet, when Aajoba had started job-hunting, he did not understand why he was treated as less than an engineer. In India back then, and probably now as well, an associate's degree seldom culminated in a successful, well-respected engineering career.

Aajoba needed to make money and send it to his family, so he took the job in the sugar factory. While he worked as a laborer, something redemptive happened that changed the course of his life. Calcutta University declared that all students who erroneously earned an associate's degree would be granted a legitimate BEE degree with full honors. And with that, Aajoba found legitimacy.

With this newly realized degree, Aajoba secured a job as an associate engineer at the power grid for Central Province (CP) and Berar British province of India. CP and Berar province is now Maharashtra and Madhya Pradesh—and are two states in central India.

Following Aajoba's footsteps, the first job title I held in engineering was associate engineer. It would take me years to learn how much his legacy influenced me. This is something I'm still discovering.

With economic stability came marriage. Aajoba married Kamal Dabke, my grandmother (Aaji), in April 1940. In my previous book, I wrote that Aaji agreed to get married on the condition that she be allowed to finish her college education. As it appears, that was not true. It was a stipulation Aajoba himself placed on the marriage proposal. He wanted an educated wife who wouldn't just spend her life in the kitchen. So even though they got married, Aaji went back to her parents' home and finished school. After graduating with a bachelor's degree in art, she moved into her husband's home.

In 1944, the pre-independence era, the CP and Berar Electric Board was looking to send a capable engineer to the U.K. for further training, because they wanted to develop local subject matter experts who could in turn coach local engineers to build up their expertise. The chairman of the board asked his administrative assistant to type a letter saying they didn't have any candidates appropriate for the training. The admin got the letter written and took it to Aajoba for proofreading, as an interim check. Aajoba read the content and told him that he would personally hand deliver the letter to the chairman.

The next morning, Aajoba went to the chairman. "I want to interview for the training position in the U.K.," he said confidently. Impressed by his boldness, the chairman granted him an interview with the board to assess whether Aajoba would qualify for the overseas training. Aajoba aced the interview, since his technical prowess was unrivaled. Just to remind you, this man had earned a gold medal at one of ten engineering colleges in India. He was exceptional, and the board offered him the opportunity—all expenses paid, transport to England, two years of training, and a ticket back home.

Aaji had recently given birth to their second child, a daughter named Jaya, who was only a couple of months old when Aajoba accepted that training opportunity. Aaji, their first child Manda, and infant Jaya all went to the train station to bid Aajoba farewell—or was it a goodbye?

Manda maushi tells me even today she remembers that scene at the train station clearly. Her father had a suitcase and garland of flowers around his neck, and her mother was inconsolable—tears streaming down her cheeks. Manda maushi said she couldn't fathom that adults cried, too.

If you're thinking this scene is a touch dramatic, think about the era. This was 1944, during World War II, and Aajoba was embarking on a fourteen-hour train journey from central India to Mumbai on the west coast. There, at Mumbai Port, he would board a ship to England. The sole purpose of this ship was to transport soldiers from this part of the world to the war front. Aajoba was one of two civilians on board.

So yes, my grandmother was beside herself. Not only was her husband leaving her with two kids for two years—but he would be traveling during wartime on a war transport vessel.

Aajoba later told his daughters about the voyage. The ship would anchor during daytime and only proceed on their route once night fell. That is the tactic they adopted for fear of German U-boat attacks. It took the vessel four months to travel from Mumbai to London, but they arrived in England unharmed.

For the next two years, Aajoba trained in electrical engineering, power electronics, power transmission lines, and electrical safety in London, Edinburgh, and Glasgow. A cherished image of the time he was in Scotland is a picture of my grandfather in a trench coat, tilted hat, and cigar in mouth. He looked like James Bond.

Upon his return, Aajoba started climbing the ranks at Madhya Pradesh Electricity Board. His British training, integrity, and intellectual capacity married to his sense of style, polished shoes, and confidence aided his career progression. Aajoba held the position of chief engineer for several years and was highly respected in his field. He wore a crisp *kurta* with gold buttons to work. A kurta is a long-sleeved tunic, which is paired with pants called *pajama*. (That's right, people, the word pajama, or *pyjama* like we call it back home, has roots in India.) In the late 1950s, Aajoba bought his first car, a Morris Motor Oxford Series III with the license plates CP C2. CP for the British province, C for car and 2 for being the second car in the province! Aajoba and another gentleman in town were the only two car owners. This make was later acquired by Hindustan Motors, and the model made popular throughout India was the Ambassador. I know Indians reading this can relate.

In moments of quiet and retrospect, I reflect on the onus of this lineage. My great grandfather raised a family in a British colony during WWI, through the Great Depression and into WWII. He rode an elephant as he collected revenue for the warlords. Aneji moved mountains to ensure his firstborn would have access to education—which culminated in Aajoba holding the position of chief engineer. That transition is unfathomable, and adding to the incredulity, Aajoba was one of two people who owned a car in Nagpur. I learned the importance of being a self-advocate from him. Throughout his college education and career, Aajoba fought his case, put his name in the hat, and asked if he could interview for the next opportunity.

While I talk about my grandfather's accomplishments, the most important life lesson he imparted was to always lead with compassion. Because even with success, Aajoba didn't forget his roots. He had a heart of gold, and at every step of his journey, he found ways to lift people up—especially the less fortunate. I think he did so because he could relate to being underprivileged. I wish I had all the stories and could write the rest of the book on him, but I only know bits and pieces.

A story of Aajoba's generosity that my aunts and mother recall is about a boy named Madhav Meshram. Madhav lived in Aajoba's childhood village and was the son of a cowherd. Madhav was being groomed to be a cowherd just like his father, while he attended primary school in the village. Aajoba found out through the grapevine that Madhav was a bright kid with a knack for numbers. Without an opportunity to go to middle and high school, and with no access to higher education, Madhav would be robbed of his full potential. Without hesitation, Aajoba approached the Meshram family and offered to take Madhav with him to Nagpur and fund the boy's education. What did Aajoba gain from this? Nothing—other than the satisfaction of giving a cowherd's family an opportunity. Education was the way out of poverty and food insecurity.

Madhav was studious and steadfast in his pursuit of a higher education. He earned a degree in engineering and found a job at the public works department (another utility company). Decades later, after Aajoba passed away, my aunts still recall how Madhav would show up at their home in a Jeep to take Aaji to the village to visit with his family. He was eternally indebted to the kindness that Aajoba showed him.

Another incident my mother often talks about is when Aajoba once stumbled—actually *stumbled*—on a man who had fainted on the side of the road. Aajoba gave him some water and asked him his name and what was going on. The man said, "*Sahib mera naam Lakshman hai, cycle rickshaw chalata hoon. Sahib, teen din se khana nahi khaya hai.*" He addressed my grandfather as sir (*sahib*) and said that his name was Lakshman, that he was a cycle-rickshaw driver, and that he hadn't eaten in three days. No further questions asked, Aajoba took Lakshman home and gave him food and water. He then offered Lakshman a job as a peon to run errands for the family; but on one condition, that he remain honest.

Honest is a such an underwhelming word in English. The word Aajoba used was *emaandaar*. To be *emaandaar* is to commit to integrity in your work, honesty in your speech, and never take what's not yours or that which hasn't been earned. Lakshman committed to *emaandaari* and spent the rest of his life with my grandparents . . . the essence of my grandfather's legacy.

Aajoba died when I was five years old. The stories I narrate are a compilation of the tales my mother and aunts told me. Aajoba also maintained diaries, where he initially wrote his life's story in Marathi and then switched to English. Maybe I get my penchant for storytelling from him!

•••

I am trying to dig into Nuwan's lineage as well. The aim is someday to explain our ancestry to our American children. I want them to know what they are made of on both sides. And I want you, as the reader, to have the context of my history—in the hopes that it will grant insight into my journey and inspire you to learn more about the impact of your lineage. I also believe we develop greater empathy (a goal of my work) when we understand the collective beauty of our diverse backgrounds.

Pagnadasa Gallege, Nuwan's father, was a young, determined twenty-three-year-old man who lived in the heart of southern Sri Lanka in his ancestral home in Ahangama. Father in Sinhalese is *Thaatha*—or *Thaathi*, more informally. Thaathi's parents took a leap of faith when they read there was a need for engineers in England. It was rumored that if you showed up at an English port, you could enroll in any engineering school, at no cost. You would only need to cover your living expenses: rent and food. Thaathi's parents pooled their savings and decided to ship off the middle child to England—literally, not figuratively. We don't quite know how Thaathi ended up enrolling in Twinkenham Polytechnic, but that is where he landed. While studying structural engineering, he shared a flat with other Sri Lankan students and worked odd jobs as his side hustle. He was astute in picking restaurant and kitchen related jobs, as he would often get leftovers, sometimes as simple as six boiled eggs, that he could then share with his flat mates. Thaathi is not much of a talker, let alone a storyteller. But one of the few stories we hear from him involves food. South Asians—we have our priorities sorted.

Already, the beauty of this story touches me—my babies get engineering from both sides. Continuing my promise of authenticity, I share with you a time when my husband was consoling our son after he slipped on some water on the floor, "Vihaan, you know why you slipped? It is called *coefficient of friction*..." I'll stop there; you can reinvent the rest of that dialogue.

Nuwan's mother's story runs parallel to Thaathi's life. Mother in Sinhalese is *Amma*, or *Ammi* more informally. Ammi's grandfather had an anglicized first and middle name, thanks to colonialism. We have a picture of this stately gentleman; he was called Charles Edward Senaratna. Mr. Charles was a wealthy timber merchant and visionary. He paid for all of his grandchildren—including the girls—to receive an English education in private school, since he knew that would be the key to a more prosperous future. Ammi was thus the recipient of his generosity.

In 1966, Ammi saw an advertisement calling for women to train and contribute to a career in nursing. There was a dearth of nurses in the U.K. that they were trying desperately to fill. Ammi, an English teacher at Sujatha Balika Vidyalaya, read the newspaper advertisement carefully and pondered, *could I become a nurse?* The offer was attractive: as long as you could pay for your transportation and make it to a British port, you would be received by educators for a full-tuition ride as well as room and board—staying in a women's hostel, getting educated in nursing, and upon graduation, starting work as a nurse. They would pay for everything, and there were no strings attached. Ammi wouldn't have to promise a stipend to them or take on debt and education loans.

The only ask was to be able to fund your way, on a ship, from Ceylon to the U.K. England needed nurses that badly. The cost of a ticket to get on a cruise liner from Sri Lanka to England was 13,000 Lankan rupees in 1966. That translates to approximately $1,000 today. It was a lot of money back then, and it still is now.

Fearless Ammi convinced her parents to let her go to England to pursue nursing. She was unmarried and had never left the country. She was now about to embark on a journey across the seas to a land unknown to become educated and pursue a career. It was the sixties. Not for a moment can I claim to understand the nerves it took to take that leap of faith. Likely she felt a mixture of uncertainty shrouded by a thin veil of eagerness in the hopes of a brighter future.

Ammi describes with nostalgia the three weeks she spent on board the Fairsky Italian Cruise. Her family could afford a ticket for her, but only in the lowest levels of the ship—in bunk-bed style arrangements with a common bath and toilets. She had 42 British pounds with her, the maximum cash allowed on your person. Ammi tells us this was much more than her parents could afford.

She was about to be the first person in her family—on either side—to leave the country. On March 5, 1966, a teary-eyed Ammi said goodbye to fifty some relatives who had all come to bid her farewell. Even now when we talk to Ammi, she says she would have enjoyed the cruise a bit more had the life journey she was embarking on not seemed so daunting. The realization that she was leaving her motherland weighed heavily on her. The cruise was but a means of transportation.

The ship had a mealtime etiquetté. Everyone was assigned a seat at a table in groups of six to eight passengers. Every day, Ammi ate with the same group—an Italian couple, a Scottish woman, and two other Sri Lankans. It didn't take long for the curiosity about having a woman from Ceylon, dressed in a saree, join them for dinner to break the ice. The intrigued Italian couple and friendly Scottish woman made their acquaintance with Ammi. She told them about life in Ceylon—about her family and plans in England. They were amazed at her courage.

The route the ship took was to navigate from the Indian Ocean to the Arabian Sea (India's western seaboard), then across the Red Sea that separates Egypt, Sudan, and Ethiopia from Saudi Arabia and Yemen. And then on to the Suez Canal in Egypt that connects the Red Sea to the Mediterranean. Then they would cross the Mediterranean along Southern Spain, go around Portugal, and finally harbor in England.

When the ship docked in the Suez Canal, many wealthier upper-level passengers planned to set foot on Egyptian land. The ship, after all, wasn't just a means of transportation; it was a cruise liner for the affluent to travel the world. Passengers had the option of purchasing a "voucher" (read: visa) to see Egypt. The voucher cost 12 British pounds.

A few days before getting to the Suez Canal, the Italian couple asked Ammi, "Ranjini, what are your plans for the stop at the Suez Canal?"

Ammi said, "I'll be transparent with you. I am carrying 42 pounds with me. I can't justify spending a third of my money on being a tourist." Her authenticity was refreshing, and without hesitation, the couple offered to pay for her voucher, insisting, "You cannot, I repeat *cannot* miss the opportunity to see the Land of the Pharaohs." Embarrassed but gracious, Ammi accepted their offer.

For context, paying 12 British pounds in the 1960s is akin to paying $250 today. Would you give that kind of money to a stranger you met on a cruise? It was a different era.

But here you have it, a Lankan woman in a saree, on a camel, seeing the wonders of Egypt. The beauty is that we still have the photograph. I don't have to imagine it, and you too can see it and marvel.

This tale of Ammi traveling by ship and sightseeing in Egypt is one of my favorite stories about her—and one I plan to recite to my children. Adventure is in our blood, on both sides. And my daughter Aarini's name in Sanskrit means *adventurous*. As she gets older, I will share her lineage with her, and we can marvel together at how daring her grandparents and great grandparents were.

I'm not quite sure how Nuwan's parents ended up in one another's social circle. But then again, I'm certain the Lankan folk found each other and stuck together. As the story goes, Nuwan's parents got married on September 20, 1969, and honeymooned in Wales.

Thaathi's career flourished in the U.K., Germany, and Belgium, while Ammi took a step back from her nursing career to raise their two children. They lived in a townhouse in Wimbledon; suffice it to say, Thaathi did well for himself. Over the years, Ammi orchestrated the immigration of two of her brothers.

This is a common immigrant story you'll hear with many families. One person ventures into the unknown and eventually aids in the move of their siblings or nieces and nephews. What I find imperative to note is that the support isn't always just monetary; it is so much more. In the sixties and seventies, immigrating from India to the U.S. as my family did—and Sri Lanka to the U.K. like Nuwan's family did—required moral support. It involved writing letters to communicate how life was in the foreign land. Sometimes it involved looking up scholarships or jobs; other times it meant providing housing for a few months while another family member such as a younger brother found a job. These were times when it took a month or longer to reach England by ship. This was not a time of internet, online forums, or social media.

But you see, this is the core of my being. There is something about the Indian culture and immigrants that has programmed fierce loyalty in me—a trait I wholly depended on during my cancer journey. That loyalty doesn't happen in isolation; it is passed through generations.

In the seventies, while the Gallege clan was raising two little ones, my paternal grandfather, Prabhakar Tamaskar, was on another journey—the opposite of immigration and growing a family. Imprisonment. I'm going to call him Dadaji for ease of following the story.

Note: Hindi gives you a different name for paternal (*Dada, Dadi*) and maternal (*Nana, Nani*) grandparents. Marathi, akin to English, uses the same word for grandparents on either side, *Aajoba* and *Aaji*. I'm using the Hindi word *Dada-ji*. "Ji" when added to a name is a sign of reverence. For example, you won't find many Indians who refer to Mahatma Gandhi as Gandhi; we call the father of our nation Gandhi-ji. And in that vein, feel free to start calling me Niyati-ji.

Dadaji was imprisoned during one of the worst periods in independent India, called The Emergency. This was a twenty-one-month period from 1975 to 1977 where Prime Minister Indira Gandhi declared a state of emergency in the country, and it was not pretty.

I want to acknowledge a moment of pride for India: we elected our first female prime minister in 1966. Many a superpower in the world still hasn't accomplished this feat. The moment of pride was balanced with a moment of reckoning for India: The Emergency under Prime Minister Gandhi was one of the darkest periods of our post-freedom history. It was marred by civil unrest, protest, and demonstrations. Note: this is a nation that takes pride in the Gandhian principle of non-violence. Yet there were mass incarcerations, and just to add some color to the chaos, why not add forced sterilizations across the country as a means of curbing overpopulation? We had it all. Arrests were made on a large scale against any political organization that opposed the ruling Congress party. Dadaji was from the opposing party.

Dadaji's 1977 jail stint wasn't his first time behind bars. Apparently, my grandfather had a penchant for standing up for civil rights and protesting political oppression. This made him a frequent flyer in the prison system. The first time he was imprisoned was in 1948, when he was in jail for five months. During this jail time, elders from the Hindu community were in prison—all educated, upstanding citizens taken away for having an opinion on their future. During those months, with nothing else to noodle on, the group of political prisoners zeroed in on the most eligible bachelor: Dadaji! Through networking, it was decided that there was a young lady *not* in prison who would be a suitable match for him. Because what else would a group of Indians do behind bars, but arrange marriages?

Soon after Dadaji was released from prison, he married Kusum Ghude, 'Dadi' on September 7, 1948. She must've known what she signed up for, as the wife of a political activist. In subsequent years, Dadaji had multiple stints in jail. Some were one-nighters, while others lasted the entirety of a weekend. But there always was a sort of faith or confidence that Dadaji would be released, it was not a state of lawlessness.

In 1977, on the final and most vocal opposition against a totalitarian government, Dadaji was imprisoned once again; but this time, it was serious. Members of the opposition parties routinely disappeared, and family members were imprisoned as well. This time, with seemingly no end in sight, Dadaji spent seventeen months behind bars. A father of five children and faithful husband, imprisoned for almost a year and a half.

How did Dadi reconcile the situation of having her husband and the father of her children in prison for participating in peaceful protests against the political party in power, using democracy as a shield to run a personal agenda?

During the years of political unrest, Dadaji became close friends with a gentleman named Atal Bihari Vajpayee, a fellow dissident of a similar age. They shared a political zeal and hope for a better tomorrow. They were patriots and wanted the best for a newly freed India. Over the next two decades, Atalji gained popularity for being an eloquent speaker. He was a writer and often recited impassioned poems that he wrote. Over time, Atalji rose to power and got elected prime minister of India.

My grandfather was close friends, or rather prison buddies, with the prime minister of India! What did that mean for us, our family connections, and our success?

Nothing.

Dadaji was incorruptible. He did not tout knowing the prime minister, nor did he ask favors from the man in power. This lesson in humility is unparalleled. Atalji was a three-term prime minister. His administration performed India's first successful nuclear testing and declared India to be a nuclear power, much to the chagrin of the rest of the world. While doing all of this in office, he found the time to fly to the town of Raipur, a few hours from where my grandparents lived in Raigarh, to visit my ancestral home. Dadi, in preparation for the visit, made a wholesome vegetarian Indian lunch and served him fresh *rotis* (round flatbread). They reminisced about their time in protest and prison, and then the prime minister left.

•••

In all that I went through—cancer, survival, learning how to give a TEDx talk on a subject I never thought I'd have to visit—I asked myself: *where did my courage come from?* In asking myself these questions, I began to unpack the stories that came before me. And I began to see a trend: that I was not the first, nor the *only* courageous one. In fact, my courage could only have come from the legacy of others before me. I share these stories with you, so that you too find the passion to explore your own stories.

I don't think Nuwan and I can ever fully comprehend how our family made it here—the sacrifices, knowing that they may not see their parents again, the boat loads of ambiguity (pun intended)—and yet they arrived. Nuwan's parents, my grandparents, and my grand-uncle, Dr. Tamasker in Cleveland, were the pioneers of our families. Standing on the shoulders of giants, I sit here in my house, looking out at our beautiful backyard, our children running around, while Nuwan tinkers with his saltwater fish tank. And I write a second book in the third language that I speak.

8. THE IMMIGRANT STORY

> "We asked for workers. We got people instead."
> —Max Frisch

Building on the family's immigration story, Nuwan and I forged our individual paths with some incredible parallels—and some dissimilarities.

Nuwan's parents moved back to Sri Lanka from England in the early 1980s, because his mother was erroneously diagnosed with multiple sclerosis. The advice given to the family was to "move to a warmer climate." It was a no-brainer for the Galleges; they would move back to Sri Lanka. With this move, the parents opted to send their kids to a public school in Colombo, Sri Lanka, called DS Senanayake. The primary language in the school was Sinhalese. After being born in London and speaking the Queen's English, Nuwan and his sister, Priyanka, were immersed in an all-Sinhalese school. And no, the parents didn't teach them conversational Sinhalese at home, so they were like fish out of water. Nuwan seldom talks about that transition, but he told me that boys bullied him because he "spoke funny."

If Thaathi had his way, he would've kept Nuwan in public school. However, Sri Lanka was about to enter a gruesome stretch of civil unrest between a misguided Janatha Vimukthi Peramuna (JVP) party and ethnic violence between the Sinhalese majority and the Tamil minority. It was a feast for all the greedy and power hungry. The JVP was a 1970s political party that was resurrected in the late eighties and was notorious for using brutal means to instill fear and submission in anyone who didn't cower to the party's agenda. JVP monopolized the news between 1987 and 1989 with their ruthless display of dominance. They wanted to make an example, and show the public what they were capable of.

Nuwan said when he was eleven or so he went on a drive with his father and saw a charred body with a burning tire around the person's neck tied to a tree. And that wasn't the first and only such sighting. This was one of the only times when Thaathi got mad at him and sternly told him, "Don't look in that direction."

Something else that Nuwan eerily remembers is *the white van*. The Lankan government was desperate to squash the JVP, so if a civilian reported that they knew someone to be a supporter of the JVP, government officials would show up in a white van and take the man of the house. People literally disappeared. The reason he remembers this is because their neighbors were recipients of this treatment. Not only did special forces take the head of the household, but they also burned the house down. The wife and children escaped, but all of their possessions were burned to the ground.

If this level of terror weren't enough, there was conflict brewing in the north between the Sinhalese and Tamils during the same period.

A brief history of the conflict: broadly speaking, there are two types of Tamils in Sri Lanka: Ceylon Tamils who migrated from India two thousand years ago, and Up Country Tamils brought by the British as slave laborers to work in the tea plantations. Tension between the two groups intensified with the introduction of communal representation by the British. You know, the old divide and conquer strategy works every time. Over time, the communal divide became more pronounced. I hate to say this, but the English really screwed up their exit strategy on the Indian subcontinent. Over time, the discord gave birth to the Liberation Tigers of Tamil Eelam (LTTE), who were a faction of Tamil Lankans who wanted their own independent country.

From the year I was born, 1983, to the year I got married to the handsome Lankan in 2009, Sri Lanka was tarnished with conflict.

Chaos ensued when the Lankan people did not know if it was the JVP, the LTTE, or the government arresting people. Sometimes bodies were found floating in a river.

India, wanting peace on the subcontinent, sent the Indian Peace Keeping Force to disband the LTTE. India had also accepted some 300,000 Tamil refugees from Sri Lanka and wanted peace in the region to stop people from fleeing.

Lawlessness eventually caused the public schools to shut down. For a few months, Nuwan and Priyanka stayed at home, but homeschooling wasn't ideal. Thaathi and Ammi caved and sent both kids to private school. Nuwan remembers a bombing that occurred less than two miles from his school. The Joint Operations Command center was bombed on a Friday, June 21, 1991, and the impact of the explosion rattled the windows of the school building. Nuwan remembers a strange detail: cobwebs descended from the ceiling, it felt like time slowed down. It is odd what the brain focuses on when it is in shock.

Irrespective of the political situation, the plan all along was to send Nuwan back to the U.K. for university. The brilliant part about schooling in England is that college-level education is free for all citizens. Let me repeat, *there is no tuition to attend university*. Nuwan studied mechanical engineering at the University of Surrey. As a British citizen, he didn't have to play the visa game. This is a game I'm all too familiar with, which I'll explore in just a bit.

•••

Nuwan's and my childhood have some important parallels. As Sri Lanka was grappling with terrorism and corruption in government, India had a similar story. An historical moment my sister remembers distinctly also happened in 1991. While it wasn't a bombing in Mumbai, it was something else of national significance. The phone rang late in the night and woke my sister. Dazed and half asleep, she saw my parents turning on the television. This was at a time when there wasn't any programming at night, but my parents had recently acquired cable television, and the BBC was reporting an incident. Priya slept on the couch, as my parents watched in disbelief.

The next morning when I woke up, I was told that the Indian Prime Minister Rajiv Gandhi had been assassinated by an LTTE suicide bomber. This act of terrorism was in retaliation for a statement made by Gandhi in an interview the previous year. Rajiv Gandhi stated that if he were reelected as prime minister, he would send more troops from the Indian Peace Keeping Force to Sri Lanka to help disarm the LTTE. Gandhi was campaigning in the southern city of Chennai when he was assassinated. Indians were enraged by the lapse in security, bereaved, and dismayed.

Nuwan tells me he, too, remembers this incident well. It was the morning after, and he was in his front yard playing, when his father returned from his morning walk, frantically waving a newspaper. Nuwan was stunned when he heard about the assassination and wondered if this would provoke retaliation from India. Nuwan tells me how he and his friends were convinced that India would descend on Sri Lanka with their navy and air force dropping bombs. The instability on the subcontinent was palpable thousands of miles across the land.

Indian armed forces did not attack our southern neighbor.

Like Sri Lanka, India, too, went through a trying phase. A few months after Rajiv Gandhi's assassination, communal riots broke out between the Hindus and Muslims there. The demolition of a mosque in northeast India by Hindu nationalists triggered the violence. The way it played out in my life, my Hindu sister and I went to a Catholic school in a predominantly Muslim part of Mumbai. My father heard about riots erupting all over the country and immediately sent the car to pull us out of class and bring us home to safety. The driver, Venkatesh, came to school and went to the principal's office, saying he had been sent to bring the Tamaskar girls home. He said that there was violence breaking out in the city, and it wasn't safe for the kids to remain in school. Sister Flory, not about to let some Hindi-speaking driver tell her how to run her school, refused to let Priya and me skip out of school.

How ridiculous is this scenario? I think about it now that I have children. If there were ever a safety concern, I would appear at Vihaan's Richards Elementary School and get him. I don't need anyone's permission.

Anyway, unbeknownst to us, the school day ended, and Priya and I made our way to the school bus. Venkatesh approached us in hysterics, saying we must leave immediately, without providing any explanation. By this point, the part of Mumbai where we were had turned violent. As we drove, Venkatesh told Priya and me to hide by the car's floorboards and not look outside. Of course, I looked outside. I spotted flames, which looked like some trash on fire. People were running aimlessly in every direction. Everything looked blurry from where we sat, as we hunkered down. I recall the sounds of muffled screams.

Our car had a little idol of Ganesha on the dashboard; most Hindus place a symbol of God on the dashboard for a safe journey. I have an idol of Ganesha in my car here in the U.S. as well. Venkatesh pulled off that idol and threw it out the window. Throwing out a symbol of God couldn't be more blasphemous, but he didn't want us to be identified as Hindus in a predominantly Muslim area. He drove like a maniac, pulling off swerves and maneuvers like never before. I don't remember how long it took us to get home, but time seemed to slow down. When we finally arrived, safely thanks to Venkatesh's bravado, Priya and I felt relief—reassured that we were out of harm's way.

Over the next few days, the government declared a curfew to bring peace and order back to the city. We missed a week of school. When things improved and we returned to school, shops reopened, and businesses were back up and running. Back in school, our teachers pretended like nothing had happened. They did not talk about the riots or ask us how we were coping.

When I reflect now on how the conflict was swept under the rug, I find it appalling, because it is not like violence of this level was commonplace. Part of the reason behind the denial and silence from the teachers and principal might have been related to religion. No one was keen to upset the hornet's nest by talking about Hindus and Muslims. But what I fail to understand is *why didn't they talk to us at a human level?* As a child, I knew that destroying shops, hurting one another, and causing physical and emotional harm was not right. They could have helped address our emotions—like fear and confusion. But this was not a decade of touchy-feely emotions.

Mumbai had not yet recovered from the aftermath of the December 1993 riots, when a powerful car bomb exploded in March 1994 at the Mumbai Stock Exchange. My father frequented the stock exchange as part of his job, yet that day he decided not to go, fatefully. We felt like he narrowly escaped and thanked the heavens for changing his plans that day. Following the bombing of the Stock Exchange building, twelve more bombs exploded throughout the city over the next two hours. The locations included the airport, Air India building, jeweler's row called

Zaveri Bazaar, a movie theater, and a fisherman's area—among others. The symbolism of this attack was clear: hurt the economic spine of the city, and target iconic buildings and locations.

Mumbai had not seen anything like this before. It was as if in those two hours, the city itself detonated. There was chaos: schools sent kids home, shops closed, local trains thronged with commuters rushing to get home—not knowing where the next bomb would be and when this would end. During this time, our friends and neighbors in our apartment complex advised my father to shave his beard. I'd always known my father with a beard, but post-bombing, they told my father that he could be targeted for looking Muslim, and hence should shave. The irony of this was that during the communal riots, we threw out an idol of Ganesha to conceal our Hinduism; now we were at risk of looking Muslim.

My father was stubborn; he did not shave his beard—a stubbornness I've proudly inherited.

Within the first twenty-four hours of the bombings, it was clear that the spirit of Mumbai could not be deterred. During the crisis, I watched the news—showing strangers pulling victims from danger and flagging cabs to take the hurt to the hospital. I don't recall discussing the evil behind those attacks, but I do remember the news reporters urging people to hold off on blood donations. This confused me, and I asked my mother, "Why are they asking blood donors to pause?"

My mother's words: "Because the blood banks are inundated."

The gravity of this remained with me. During a time where Mumbai-*kars* didn't know which part of the city would be attacked next, they rushed to blood banks to donate.

The aftermath of the thirteen bombings was the shutdown of schools, again, and restricted hours for grocery stores with a strict curfew. This lasted a month, maybe more, before Priya and I returned to school.

•••

It feels like serendipity, a hand of destiny, that Nuwan and I met. The troubles our respective countries saw were intertwined at some point—India and Sri Lanka are neighbors—yet we met across the world in the metropolis of Peoria, Illinois. I often say my life is a culmination of brilliant coincidences, but there has been nothing more spectacular than the fate that brought Nuwan and me together.

When Nuwan and I got married in December 2009, the wedding was my first visit to Sri Lanka. The government had put an end to the LTTE reign, and it was a bloody end with a tremendous loss of civilian lives. In the wake of the end of the civil war, Sri Lanka reopened tentatively. I say that because upon departing the airport, five minutes into our drive, there was a checkpoint. At the checkpoint was a young man, seeming barely out of his teenage years, in a military outfit, armed with an AK-47, pulling cars over for a security check. In all the years back home in Mumbai, and the violence we witnessed or heard about in the news, I had never seen a gun, let alone an AK-47!

A feeling of powerlessness came over me—which starkly contrasted with what transpired around me. Nuwan's father chatted with the young soldier in Sinhalese. There were smiles, and then he looked in the back to check out Nuwan and me.

Nuwan told him, "This is my wife; she is from India," in Sinhalese. With heightened senses, I hung onto every word Nuwan said and committed it to memory, sort of like a defense arsenal.

Thirty minutes down the road, we got pulled over again, and the same scenario was repeated. However, this time around, I said to Nuwan, "I got this, honey." Then with a great big smile, I said to the army man, "*Mama India-ve, mage mahatye Sinhala.*"

The driver, Nuwan's father, Nuwan, and the soldier started laughing—and exchanged looks of amazement. A bit of charm never hurts!

It seems foreign to me now to look back at our childhoods. *How did we live through those years of turmoil and violence?* Acknowledging full well that we were physically unharmed and our families were safe, I still cannot for a moment fathom raising our children in a turbulent environment. My children are citizens of the U.K. and the U.S.A. I wonder what immigration journey they will embark upon. Meanwhile, I will tell them all about our respective journeys (minus the gore and violence).

•••

With the parallels in our upbringing and childhood experiences, there is a point of dissimilarity. My immigrant journey has been a tad different from my man's. I came to the United States on something called the F1 visa.

Let's start by acknowledging that that is a pretty awesome visa category: F1, like Formula1. I felt the clout of a race car driver—invincible.

So, this F1 visa allowed me to be a full-time student at Ohio State University, with the generous freedom to work part-time. I worked twenty hours a week at the ElectroScience Laboratory as a research assistant. Upon graduating, I applied for a permit called Optional Practical Training (OPT), which could be used if I got hired. "Big Yellow" (code name for the first Fortune 500 company that hired me, I doubt you can crack it) hired me based on my electrical engineering degree, my interview skills, and well . . . this OPT card.

An OPT is only valid for a few months. Then the employer needs to apply for a work permit for the immigrant employee. The work permit, H1B, has an annual cap.

United States Citizenship and Immigration Services (USCIS) back then permitted some 55,000 H1B visas per annum. Companies across the U.S. that hired foreign nationals legally needed to procure an H1B for their immigrant employee within that limit of 55,000.

When the number of applicants exceeds the visa capacity, which happens recurrently, the government uses a lottery system to decide who gets an H1B. To entrust your future to a lottery system, that is the kind of uncertainty some of us immigrants face.

I was granted an H1B on my first attempt, which permitted me to work legally in America for three years. After three years, I would need to renew the H1B for another three years, and at the six-year mark, the visa would expire. At that point, I would have three options: go back to university and reacquire that F1 visa, return home, or get my employer to apply for my permanent residency—called the green card.

I was on my second round of an H1B visa and one year into our marriage when we decided to emigrate to the U.K., back to Nuwan's country of citizenship. It was an exciting move but it meant I would need to learn a new immigration system and terminology. Our first task was to apply for a spousal visa for me to legally live and work in England. Nuwan and I reviewed the requirements—including the evidence needed, the application form, and the application fee. The process was to provide evidence, and then we would be called for a joint interview as a couple.

A crucial part of the application was submitting evidence of a legitimate marriage with the intent of staying married. One of the things the U.K. is wary of is a marriage of convenience—instances when a citizen marries an immigrant as a business deal, then once the immigrant spouse gains citizenship, the couple gets divorced.

Nuwan and I needed to prove the authenticity of our relationship. Based on what we read in forums online, we created a binder of information—only since we are engineers, it was more like the mother of all binders. It was thorough, indexed, color tabbed, and massive. I will not go over the amount of detail we shared with Her Majesty's immigration department; let's just say it was over the top.

After submitting the evidence, we waited eagerly for the interview date. And waited. They had my passport; there is something nerve-racking about not having your passport in hand when you're an immigrant in a country. I felt uneasy the whole time.

One day, we received a big package in the mail from the embassy. They sent the binder back to us. I thought they would use it in the interview, to quiz me on dates and such. My heart was pounding as we opened the folder. The embassy returned all the documents *and my passport* with a letter.

This was not a good sign. I was supposed to get an interview date, but instead they sent everything back.

The letter stated that I had been granted the spousal visa! They didn't even want to interview us. Nuwan and I were beside ourselves, laughing to the point of hysterics. The binder was probably like nothing they'd seen before—the detail, the tabs, the index, our very first e-mail exchange, the engagement story, the visit to my alma mater, our families meeting for the first time, copies of air tickets, marriage photos from both India and Sri Lanka. We topped it all with two letters of reference—one from my lawyer-roommate Jen, and another from Nuwan's dear friend Miguel.

I think they had seen enough. I can only imagine them rolling their eyes at seeing all the evidence.

There are some perks to being engineers who thrive on attention to detail.

•••

On a spousal visa, once gainfully employed and working in England, I had another deadline to watch. The spousal visa comes with an expiration date, after which you need to apply for the British version of the green card called Indefinite Leave to Remain (ILR). The application is rather straightforward, nothing like the folder we had created for the visa. But there is a test that I needed to pass to get the ILR, called Life in the U.K. Test.

To prepare for the exam, I purchased the *Life in the U.K.* book, a 145-page thriller broken up into five chapters. My favorite chapter was chapter three, titled "A long and illustrious history." The irony of the chapter title was not lost when I learned about the Black Death (which is about as fun as it sounds), the War of the Roses (which is not at all what it sounds like), the turbulent Middle Ages, clansmen uprising, and more. The pages are a narrative packed with the names of kings and queens, invasions, and dates back to 55 B.C. I had to cram a lot of information into an already packed brain, as I spent my days working on the combustion control of natural gas engines. This historical data was using up precious grey matter that I needed for my day job.

But I did the needful and passed the test. With this milestone, I was now a permanent resident of the U.K.

Life would be all too simple for me if I had gotten British citizenship and we had lived happily ever after in Royal Leamington Spa. But we decided, *why not return to America?*

This time around in the U.S., there was a new visa for me: the elite L1 visa granted to experienced professionals. You can guess how the story goes; the L1 visa also expires over the course of a few years. It was getting to the point where I needed to be on a status without an expiration date. I spoke to my HR manager to start my permanent residency process. And thus, we embarked on the green card quest, which in our unique situation was a quick process. Six months from the time of application, we got our green cards. My husband and I are permanent residents in a country where our children are citizens—in the United States. The green card is in fact permanent—for as long as we reside in this great nation. I am so done (famous last words, watch as we move again and I need another visa). I am *so done* with being in a citizenship vortex.

In the middle of 2020, after five years of permanent residency, Nuwan and I applied for our U.S. citizenship. And in 2021 we were naturalized as citizens.

•••

At the start of my immigration journey, I was acutely aware of the visa hoops of fire I needed to jump through. Consequently, I developed antipathy toward people who crossed the border illegally and were granted citizenship—without waiting in queues or jumping through those visa hoops. In my misguided, entitled brain, I thought it wasn't fair. *Everyone should wait in line and earn their right to a life in America, just like I did,* ran through my mind.

Something to note, the green card in the U.S. is granted on an antiquated quota system. The quotas are based on the applicant's visa category and nationality. The fancier the visa category, meaning a visa that is for specialized professions and industry experts, the shorter the wait. In the nationality quota, there are four countries that are on epic backlogs and thus have long processing times. No prizes for guessing

India, China, and Mexico. What surprised me was that the fourth nation on this list is the Philippines. I know fellow Indians who are on green card waitlists for over a decade. Anecdotally, getting it within seven to eight years is considered timely. I argue, *why should others get to jump the line?*

I am ashamed to admit that I had a lapse in empathy. Instead of putting myself in the shoes of a family that has fled their homeland, leaving their worldly belongings behind, traveling hundreds if not thousands of miles with the hope of safety, no prospects in mind other than refuge—instead of empathy, I was sour. I felt asylum seekers had an advantage in the system. All I can do now is shake my head in dismay at not having greater perspective on human suffering. Over the years, I educated myself on the plight of asylum seekers and the unprincipled coyotes they pay to get them across the border. Even after paying the smuggler, there are reports of many migrants left behind to die en route to the border. And these are the cases of those crossing over land, by foot. Then there is arrival by boat and dinghy. The courage it must take to cross the open ocean, even when it is common for sea-crossing refugees not to know how to swim. On a larger global scale, there are the cross-continent refugees who escape war zones by any means possible. The best analogy I can come up with is this: It is like going to the ER for a sprained ankle and being disgruntled that a person with a gunshot wound is being attended to first.

How, even in a moment of weakness, could I ever think that this lot had an advantage? What I described to you—my visa dance, as I like to call it—stems from privilege, the privilege of coming from an affluent family that could afford to send me to the United States for my undergraduate education. The privilege that then paved the way for hard work, earning me a degree, and landing me a job that would sponsor my visa. Twenty years later (but who is counting?), and I am finally a citizen.

If you're a citizen of this great nation who is feeling bitter about immigrants stealing jobs, or don't have an appreciation for the risks refugees take, I feel you may be having a lapse-in-empathy moment. I hope my narrative makes you pause and reconsider. Geographically—where you are born; racially, to which set of parents; economically, to affluence or poverty, to adoring parents or abandonment—is the ultimate *embryonic lottery*. If you've hit the jackpot or won that lottery, how are you using that privilege?

9. FAR FROM HOME

> "The ache for home lives in all of us. The safe place where we can go as we are and not be questioned."
> —Maya Angelou

You now have a glimpse of *who* I come from. But to truly understand me is to know more about *where* I come from—and how that plays out in the American chapter of my life, and the entirety of my adulthood away from the homeland. In learning about the geography behind my family's history, I also hope it will pique your interest in your own heritage. By understanding our rich and diverse backgrounds, we can better achieve the goal of expanding empathy for all.

First a little history lesson, grab a coffee.

India is the third largest country in Asia; only the behemoths of Russia and China precede us in size. India has twenty-two official languages, the highest of any country in the world. This diversity in language translates into diversity of her people. While we are one race—labeled as South Asian or Asian geographically—we are in fact many shades of brown. Within the spectrum of brown, we have eyes that are hazel, dark brown, green, and occasionally blue. My sister has green-brown hazel eyes. Hair texture also varies by region (pre-processed natural hair, that is); there's wavy, poker straight, stringy curls, and everything in between. While hair color is primarily black, we also have brown hair—a color my sister and niece visibly share.

India boasts of diversity in religion as well. India is the birthplace of the world's oldest religion, Hinduism. I am a practicing Hindu. India is also the birthplace of Buddhism and Jainism. My husband is Buddhist, making our children…. *Bindus*? If Buddhist Hindus start calling themselves Bindus, note that you read it here first! (Play on words, *bindu* also means dot in Hindi; akin to the dot we wear on our foreheads in India.)

India had an influx of foreign religions. One of the first foreign religions to reach the motherland was Judaism, around a couple of thousand years ago. Unlike in other parts of the world, Jews have enjoyed a haven in India with relatively non-existent instances of anti-Semitism. It amazes me to think that one of the iconic symbols of Hinduism is the Swastika, which the Nazis then turned upside down—literally and metaphorically. The Hindu swastika derives from the words *su*, meaning good, and *asti*, which means to exist—which when put together, symbolizes well-being. In India even today, you will find the correct swastika—and the sentiment behind it—drawn above front doors or entryways. The Nazi version of it is backwards and tilted to its side. Jewish Indians know that this symbol was sacred to Hinduism long before its misappropriation. Jews hold a special place of mutual respect in Indian society.

I *know* my children will have questions, once they learn about the Holocaust and the misappropriation of a sacred Hindu symbol. I wonder if Hindus outside the homeland shy away from having a swastika in the house, because of the ugly European history behind it.

There's another religion that was driven out of the Middle East as Islam took a strong hold in the region. India provided shelter to Zoroastrians—

Persians who fled their homeland of Iran to escape persecution in 600 CE (Common Era). Colloquially, this set of Zoroastrians is known as Parsis, stemming from being Persian or Iranian, the obvious etymology. A famous Parsi you might know about is Freddy Mercury, the lead singer of Queen. A prominent Parsi family in India is the Tata family. While it might be impressive to point out that Tata Motors now owns Jaguar Land Rover, for me a prized contribution from this Iranian family is the Tata Memorial Hospital and Tata Cancer Center in Mumbai.

Islam was brought to India by Arab traders, which paved the path for the Mughal rule (think Taj Mahal). Today, Islam is the second largest religion in India. Christianity took root in India, too—the timeline of which is highly debated. But the spread in such a vast country was more palpable when Portuguese explorers reached India in the late fifteenth century.

I feel it is imperative to understand the extent of diversity in India. It was an ancient melting pot where religions were born, immigrants and refugees arrived on foot or by boat, and foreign religions were allowed to thrive. I take pride in Indian history.

With a myriad of languages and an amalgamation of colloquial and foreign cultures, there is one thing that doesn't add up: India's obsession with skin color. I'll be more specific—the Indian bias towards fair, light, and pale skin. We call it *gora*, meaning white in Hindi. Children in India quickly pick up on this preference to be light-skinned. It starts with mothers telling their kids, "Don't play outside in the sun; you'll get dark." It festers when a grandparent picks the lightest grandchild as their favorite. Let's just say the Snow White fairy tale with the line, "Mirror, mirror, on the wall, who's the fairest of us all?" meant just that to Indian parents.

Who is the fairest of them all? Siblings, cousins, classmates—pitted against each other on the basis of skin tone.

The beauty and wellness industry was quick to pick up on the *gora* fixation. I present to you, one of the leading facial moisturizers in India, called Fair and Lovely. The cream is touted to have a skin-lightening formula with guaranteed success. Commercials on television display results by showing a before-and-after. Before: the damsel was in distress with her coffee-colored face. She wondered if she would ever find a suitor. After using Fair and Lovely, the destitute woman now has lighter skin and gets to choose from multiple marriage offers. At some point, the men felt jilted and voiced their dismay, so the company came up with a new product for men, Fair and Handsome. Use Fair and Handsome, and change your life from being a stunt-double to being the lead action hero. I am paraphrasing the commercials we watched growing up. Over time, the cheesy eighties advertisements were replaced by top celebrities and endorsements from Bollywood stars. The creams these days even come with shade cards, so the user can track the lightening of his or her skin.

Full disclosure: I happen to be on the fair-pale side of the spectrum. Which means I once enjoyed a bit of favoritism. I got more compliments than I think I deserved, and I wasn't discouraged from wearing brightly colored clothes. Because, as they said, "Anything looks good on your coloring." While I write about this topic, I want to be transparent and tell you I was not the subject of discrimination on skin color, rather a recipient of its privilege.

Subliminal messaging was strong during my childhood, when the lead actors for a movie were chosen from the lightest brown pallet and the bad guy was dark chocolate. In kids' cartoons and nursery rhymes, the thief who stole candy was portrayed by a dark brown character. But what really brought the message home was when the lightest of brown girls was picked for the lead role in a school play, purely based on how white she looked.

Being dark skinned is not an equal opportunity curse. Dark girls have it harder than their counterpart dark boys. Because if there's a way society can make it harder on women, we find it. Having a daughter with a touch of brown pigmentation, which is natural for the subcontinent, is a cause of worry for parents. *Who will want to marry a dark girl? To get her married we will need a sizeable dowry.* I call it buying "*gora* credit." Here's a darker girl, throw in a big sum of money and gold, and like magic, she is marriage worthy. Another phrase often used about darker girls is, "She has nice features." When you hear that a girl has "nice features," it is code for, "she is dark."

Dark boys don't have it easy by any means, but they have it easier than girls. Parents will overcome their son's darkness by touting that the son is "successful," and the family is "well-off." People often say, *kala hai par dil to saaf hai*—which translates to, "He is dark, but his heart is pure." How damaging is that sentence?

Way back when, darker skin was associated with manual labor and jobs that were exposed to the elements. Pale skin was a sign of privilege and hence carried social prestige.

After moving to the United States, something wonderful happened: I came to the realization that no matter how light-skinned a brown person is, they will never be white. I also learned that there are other East Asian cultures that share a similar obsession with whiteness. There is a broad bucket created for us, called "persons of color" or "non-white." While the non-white category is all-encompassing, it can be a great equalizer for people of South Asian descent.

Being fair skinned took a back seat and offered me no undeserved advantage in America. I lost my fair skin privilege and I believe that was a good thing for my personal growth. The conversations I've participated in that address race are generally around the great divide between white and black. More inclusively, some discussions touch on the perspective of *black, indigenous, people of color* (**BIPOC**).

But here, I offer you another viewpoint. Depending on a person's cultural, ethnic, or immigrant background, some have witnessed deep levels of discrimination within their native communities. When we move to the Western world, those differences are often moot, and the move can level the playing field.

•••

That is not to say that the Western world does not also have its distinct and grave challenges in relation to skin color and race, to which numerous American news reports and individual experiences can attest. I don't have enough space to devote to all of those challenges here, but I will explore a bit of what it was like to be an Indian woman integrating into a male-dominated field in the U.S. culture—with other Asians. The more I see, the more I can understand others.

While I was a student at the Ohio State University, my undergraduate engineering classes looked like a boy's club. Out of a class of 200 pursuing a sophomore to junior-level electrical and computer engineering course, generally speaking, you would have 196 pimple-faced white boys, one brave Caucasian girl, and three women of color. In the early 2000s, at the largest state school in the United States, I didn't know a single black female engineer. The three women of color in any given class were Asian: Chinese, Indian, or Pakistani. (I am oversimplifying the identities of the women of color for the sake of the narrative and using anecdotal data and my memories of undergrad.)

Immigrant women of color were few and far between in my field. I happened to make the acquaintance of two Pakistani girls—Tooba and Shumaila—both pursuing their undergraduate degrees like I was.

Tooba was betrothed to a Pakistani man, only a few years older than her. Between the two families, it was decided that they would let Tooba go to the United States to pursue her education—with a firm promise, rather a contract, that she would return and marry the young man.

Shumaila was a free bird of sorts, tied not to a man, but to Tooba's fate. She was to chaperone Tooba during the four years of university, be her roommate, and ensure that she didn't veer from the path back to her suitor.

When I first gravitated toward brown girls who looked like me, they were the first Pakistanis I had ever met. That is correct, a region that was united for thousands of years only recently divided into two countries by our colonial warlords, yet it took my moving halfway across the world to meet my neighbors.

When our group started getting to know each other, I realized something intrinsic. We had more similarities than differences. Their communication styles, word inflections, and nuances were familiar. Some of our mannerisms were the same, too. We grew up respecting our elders, and we attached terms of reverence to our older siblings. We shared the same enthusiasm for spices and chai; our culinary journeys weren't that divergent. Adding to this, I was acutely aware that while I came from a male-dominated society, they came from a *principally* male-dominated society. If I stood up against misogyny, they were valiant warriors against it and broke the mold. I respected my Pakistani sisters.

Tooba and Shumaila formed a strong bond with me. We studied together, did our laboratory work together, went to office hours and worked on tough homework assignments together. The highlight, however, was when Tooba and Shumaila taught me how to make authentic *biryani*—a dish with meat, rice, vegetables, and abundant spices. People, Indian biryani is good, Indian Muslim biryani is exemplary, Pakistani biryani—forget it;

it's a world apart. The girls lived in an apartment, while I lived in a shared duplex with my American roommates who were away on holiday. It was my opportunity to learn from the master chefs, so I invited them over for a biryani lesson. Tooba brought most of the spices, and I provided rice, yogurt, cilantro, and some other paltry ingredients. That evening, I had the best biryani of my life, hands down—mouth-watering, binge-on-biryani-till-you-pass-out good.

I cannot pinpoint what it was about my friendship with the pair that changed something in me, but it did. I was able to put a face to my adversary, and that humanized them. We really aren't that different. I didn't ask, but have always wondered if Tooba and Shumaila felt the same. *Will they consider Indians in a different light?*

The thing is, growing up in South Mumbai, I was surrounded by homogeny of sorts. While I boast about diversity in India, I grew up with people who worshiped like me. Living in the affluent area of South Mumbai meant that I was surrounded by friends whose parents had comparable educational backgrounds to my parents. Moving away from home, I went from favored to minority, and interacting with other people from the subcontinent helped me grow. My exposure and subsequent growth started small; I tried to become more cognizant of the plight of my Muslim friends. I started by asking my friend, Yohan, about any discrimination he might have faced in Mumbai. All along, I was 100 percent sure that since he was an educated Muslim who held a respectable job, he would not be subject to prejudice.

Yohan's persona is rather unique. He is a product of a Muslim father and a Christian mother, and he identifies as Muslim. He is married to a half-Hindu, half-Christian woman who identifies as Christian.

Yohan told me the issues he had finding an apartment in Mumbai. *In my city, how could that be? Cash is king; surely rupees forked out by a Hindu couple would have the same value as rupees from a non-Hindu couple.* It appeared landlords and sellers did not want Muslim tenants or buyers, and they were clear about it to Yohan. He struggled to find a place, despite having the money and resources to pay up front. At the height of his frustration, Yohan told his real estate agent, "Only show me a flat if I can actually buy it. If the seller thinks a Muslim and his Christian wife are unfit, don't take us there." The realtor suggested that they go with his wife's half-Hindu status and say they were a "Hindu couple." Yohan flat-out refused. After an excruciating process of rejection based on religion, they finally found a place in a high-rise.

It's important to note that in the rental market in India, landlords tend not to like single women as tenants. A single woman living away from her parents and unmarried is seen as promiscuous. *Who knows what kind of men will frequent her bed?* This is part of the age-old tarnishing of women as being salacious if not tied down.

I want to proudly share that we have a flat in Mumbai that is rented out to tenants, and for a stretch of eight years, it was occupied by a single lady—a powerhouse of a woman who worked in the financial district there. My mother would never discriminate against an independent single woman.

While I was aware of how female tenants were treated, I lacked the capacity to expand this to other minorities. I needed to open my eyes and be conscious of my city's underbelly.

In the continued effort toward full disclosure, I'm all about "let's hold hands and sing Kumbaya," as long as we don't bring India-Pakistan cricket into the mix. Cricket is often dubbed as the national religion of India, and we as a people are passionate about watching the national team perform on the international stage. When there's an India-Pakistan match, our biggest rival, offices unofficially close for the day, or employees come in just to watch the match on the big screen with colleagues.

This also holds true in my marriage. India-Sri Lanka cricket matches are also a passionate event in the Tamaskar-Gallege house. On April 2, 2011, the two countries battled it out on the cricket field for the Cricket World Cup. Our household was its own battle ground. Nuwan's uncles, aunts, and cousins appeared at our rental home in Long Itchington with massive Sri Lankan flags, and we placed bets on the outcome: If India wins, Nuwan has to make me a three-course meal and do dishes for a week. If Sri Lanka wins, I'm the cook and dishwasher. Let's just say I had a wonderful dinner and a week of not doing dishes.

Sidebar: if *Long Itchington* made you snicker, I know a little bit about your maturity.

•••

From standing out, to wanting to fit in, to realizing it is better to stand out, to remembering how important it is to fit in—I'm a hot mess of who I am and who I should be. But I learned another humble lesson about my skin color and race during my undergraduate years.

My first experience of racial profiling occurred in December 2003, when I went on a road trip with three other college buddies. We drove from Ohio to Texas. The plan was to go to Big Bend National Park, camp out there for a few nights, then make our way to North Padres Island for beach camping. We were poor college students, and camping offered the best of both worlds—an opportunity to be in nature, at a minimal cost.

As we made our way to Big Bend National Park, without GPS but using old-school maps, I realized that the park is in the middle of nowhere. It's a good two hundred miles away from civilization and on the U.S.-Mexico border. Not surprisingly, we were stopped by border patrol on the way to the park. The border patrolman looked past my three white friends and locked his gaze on me. "I need you to step out of the car, ma'am," he said. I had never been called *ma'am* before. *How polite!* I stepped out, and my friends got out, too, to stretch their legs.

Then I was ushered into the border control office, a glorified tent.

Texas border patrolmen are well versed with the brown people coming from south of the border, and these patrolmen figured that wasn't where I came from. But to my disadvantage, they mistook me for a person of Middle Eastern descent. Post 9/11, being brown raised an alarm, which was unfortunate. They sat me down for some questioning. I was asked the basics: name, date of birth, address, purpose of visit, Social Security number, etc. I was a law-abiding immigrant studying engineering at Ohio State University. I had my Social Security number, a driver's license, and a verifiable address. I figured I was good to go.

But something about my answers didn't satisfy them, and they told me, "Special Agent Cody"—can't make this up—"has been summoned to cross-examine you." This is when I started to worry. *What in the world was I doing here? How come*—rhetorical question—*they don't want to question my white mates?* Special Agent Cody arrived a half hour later, apologized for the delay, saying that he was in the middle of taking family photographs, and then jumped straight to the questioning.

First Question: "What is your religion?"

What? Are they allowed to ask me this? Don't question it; you might get in trouble.

"I am Hindu."

Second Question: "Are you Muslim?"

Is this a trick question? Don't be snarky, just answer.

"No, sir, I am Hindu. That is not Muslim. It is pretty much the opposite of Muslim."

I'll admit it wasn't my finest moment, but I wanted separation between me and the 9/11 terrorists.

Third Question: "Are you a terrorist, or have you taken part in any terrorist activities?"

Umm, this escalated quickly. I'm an engineering student traveling with some nerds to go camping. Check the car. It has tents, sleeping bags, and like eight pairs of clothes.

I respond, "No, sir, I am not a terrorist."

Fourth Question, just to drive the point home: "Are you a suicide bomber?"

Seriously, can't make this shit up. Now I'm thinking I'll be in jail somewhere, not able to tell my mother why I was such an idiot to go to Texas for camping.

"No, sir, I am not a suicide bomber."

There was a knock on the door. My heart skipped a beat; no, I think it stopped beating completely. Another agent popped his head in and said, "She checks out."

Special Agent Cody stepped out briefly. I was able to breathe again.

My man Cody came back and said, "I apologize for the delay. When we were pulling up your details, the agent had your first and last names reversed. Everything looks good; you are free to go. Enjoy camping." *Holy mother of Ganesha*, I was free to leave.

When I walked out of the tent, I watched my buddies: one throwing rocks over a barbed-wire fence, another checking tire pressure, and one conversing with a pair of patrolmen. There was an undeniable lack of severity in their mood. I asked my friends what the patrolmen said to them. Apparently, they were warned about jail time for harboring and transporting an illegal alien. To which Adrian valiantly said, "She's not an alien, man."

The next lesson I learned about living away from the motherland was a sobering encounter with racial profiling. My shade of brown was not quite the right shade.

•••

While my Hindu identity has come up a few times, as it did with border patrolmen in Texas, there is one thing I don't often discuss with others. Hinduism used to be steeped heavily in a four-tier caste system. Casteism still exists but has started to blur its boundaries.

First, I want to point out that the caste system is not unique to India. It is practiced in Japan, Korea, Sri Lanka, Tibet, and Myanmar. And I won't be surprised if it exists in other parts of the world, too. Nuwan tells me even the elephants in Sri Lanka are segregated by caste.

In Hinduism, *Brahmins* are the highest caste, comprised of priests and scholars. It is followed by the warrior caste, called *Kshatriya*. The merchants and artisans are the next level down, known as the *Vaishya* caste. The lowest caste is the *Shudras*, comprising laborers.

While the middle two castes—warriors and merchants—didn't seem to change in status much over time, Brahmins enjoyed a higher degree of privilege, and Shudras were left with menial jobs like cleaning gutters and toilets and handling animal carcasses. These jobs were considered unclean and polluting, hence this caste over time came to be known as the *untouchables* or *Dalits*. If the work was unclean, one must not be close to the class of people doing it.

Way back when, the treatment of Dalits could be summarized in two words: segregation and prohibition. Dalit children were expected to go to segregated schools. Dalits were prohibited from drinking water from the same well as other castes. They were not allowed to eat with other castes or walk on the same streets. Belonging to the Dalit caste pretty much guaranteed you would be on the lowest socio-economic level—and would stay there for generations.

I am not going to spell it out here, but I'm certain that the parallels to U.S. history jump out at you.

However, unlike race, which can be deduced from physical features, you might wonder how caste is identified. For the most part, you can determine the caste of a person by their last name. Surnames are regional; I can tell if someone is from north or south India. And most Indian grandmothers pass on the knowledge of recognizing caste by last name.

Post-independence, India made an audacious effort to remove the Dalit curse. In 1950, India instituted affirmative action, making it illegal to discriminate on the basis of caste. India created a quota system in education and reserved a set number of government jobs for Dalits. One of the first affirmative action policies in the world, it is called the Scheduled Caste and Scheduled Tribe (SCST) Act, which protects groups of lower caste folk who all fall under the Dalit umbrella.

As it was with the color of my skin—being light brown—my family also belongs to the highest caste, Brahmins. As I became mature enough to understand quotas, I had a primordial reaction to affirmative action. Because when you're privileged, equality smells a bit like unfairness. I was but a child. Coping with the loss of my father, I was at capacity and unable to find an ounce of empathy for the historically oppressed class.

Guess what moving to the United States did for me? My Brahmin caste is irrelevant now. It means nothing to my friends, colleagues, job applications, or social capital. The only place where it would still matter is in marriage. I married a tall drink of water who is a Sri Lankan Buddhist, so that debate is silenced.

Now away from my home country, I started educating myself about the history of untouchables in India. The beauty of that exercise was that it spurred reading of other historical novels about the treatment of other oppressed classes. I read books about Koreans in the Japanese empire, Black books written by Black authors to understand the narrative through their perspective, books on or by Holocaust survivors, refugee stories about escaping Afghanistan during the Russian invasion, and the list goes on. I find myself drinking from a bottomless well. While I am no scholar of the history behind these stories, I cannot say I wasn't aware. And with that awareness comes responsibility. It is my responsibility to practice empathy.

•••

Ohio State University was my introduction to America, and it cushioned the blow. I had been convinced that watching *The Simpsons* prepared me for a life in the Midwest. And that strategy seemed to pan out. I suffered from a mild case of culture shock in the first week of being at Ohio State but quickly got accustomed to new mannerisms and societal norms. I assimilated.

The advantage was that at the undergraduate level, I was surrounded by students my age. Everyone was in the same boat, away from home, and thrown into the unfamiliar territory of living in the dorms. Being in the honors engineering dorm meant that I was part of the nerd-herd, and I fit right in. For my dorm mates, my name wasn't a hindrance; it was an enabler to endless conversations about my background. I essentially lived in a bubble.

However, one sunny day in 2005, I graduated, took up a job in the real world, and my bubble burst.

When I started working, I desperately wanted to fit in. As a young, non-white, female engineer in a predominantly white male environment, I stuck out like a sore thumb. I didn't need a complicated first name to further differentiate me. Work was nothing like school. All of my friends at Ohio State had pronounced my name with ease. At work in Peoria, Illinois, managers asked me if I had a nickname. The comments that stuck with me were the off-hand declarations, "I'm never going to remember that," or, "Can I call you Ni instead?" I wanted to avoid unnecessary attention, so I decided to give myself a pronounceable nickname. With a mindless everyone-else-does-it justification, I whitewashed my name for ease of pronunciation, like my comrades. Nikhil becomes Nik; Dakshineshwar becomes Daks.

The name I adopted was Nina. I don't know what says identity crisis more than changing your name. But I was twenty-one and grateful to land a job in a Fortune 500 company that would sponsor my visa. I wanted to fit in.

The problem with the ad hoc name change is that I was unsuccessful at retraining my brain to respond to Nina. Colleagues would say "Hey Nina!" in the hallway, and I would simply continue doing my own thing without responding. The name change didn't work for me, and to be honest, I felt like a sellout. My name wasn't Nina, and I had never been called that. A month of mental gymnastics later, I sheepishly told my manager, John, that I needed to revert to Niyati, because "no one has ever called me Nina." It was embarrassing. But I knew I had to undo what I had started.

I had heard that the formation of one's identity is among the most significant milestones in a person's life. I had an identity; heck, I had a solid one. I rehashed—*I'm an engineer, immigrant, and female; I'm five foot something on a good day, small but feisty, and my name is Niyati.* How did I get to twenty-one and become uncertain of my name? My name! With whatever courage I had left, I came clean, asked for a new badge, changed my name back to Niyati, and never looked back.

Fifteen years into my career, my name is still not an enabler. A couple of months ago, I was in a teleconference with a new team. The coordinator called each person by first name and asked for introductions, "Jim, would you like to introduce yourself and tell us about your background?" Everyone got their turn, and when it came to me, he said, "Would the person from Cummins like to introduce themselves?" Let me tell you, worse than mispronouncing someone's name is not saying it at all.

Albeit inconvenient for most, I have come to realize how cool it is to have a unique name. While working at Big Yellow, I was the only Niyati amongst 90,000 employees, and the last I checked, I am still the only Niyati in Columbus.

Never go by Nina or something easy just to fit in. It is better to stand out, always, than to morph who you are just to fit the mold.

Also, have the courage to fess up to an identity crisis, and you will recover from it.

• • •

It was an unusually cold, fall evening in September 2017. I had big plans for a Friday night. Nuwan would stay home with the kids, so I could attend a "Cooking Across Cultures" event at a local church. The guest cooks were two local Pakistani women who would teach us to cook biryani! I was coming full circle. The chef extraordinaire introduced herself as Mahvish; she was accompanied by a couple of Pakistani girlfriends who were sous chefs. I loved their beautiful traditional attire, like the Indian *salwar kurta,* distinct with their beautiful pastel shades and regal embroidery.

As Mahvish finished preparing the meal, she bade us farewell, telling us she had to go root for her son's football team. I thought to myself: *Could this be more American? A Pakistani woman does a cooking class in the basement of a local church, attended by citizens and immigrants—only to rush to watch her high school son play football at the Colts stadium.* That evening carries cherished memories for me, and the biryani was the cherry on top.

Less than a year after the Cooking Across Cultures event, in June 2018, I rang the bell to commemorate the end of chemotherapy. Everyone at the cancer center came out of their bunkers, into the hallway to cheer the patient on. The end of chemotherapy is a significant milestone; it is not always the end of treatment but a milestone that is recognized. I rang the bell…

Three times well
Its toll to clearly say
My treatment's done
The course is run
And I am on my way.

I was overcome but holding back tears. As I was walking away, I made eye contact with a familiar face. It was Mahvish!

Mahvish is a pharmacist at the cancer center. When she saw me, even though I was bald, she immediately remembered me from the church cooking event. Her eyes welled up. She said, "I had no idea it was you…" She hugged me, but I couldn't look her in the eyes. I thought I would fall apart. I felt vulnerable and exposed. She was the only person at the cancer center who had seen me pre-cancer. Everyone else there had met me upon diagnosis.

During a follow-up appointment to discuss my radiation plan with Dr. Madhatter McMullen, Mahvish asked the nurses to convey a message to me asking if it was alright for her to visit me in the consultation room. Of course, I said yes.

A few minutes later, Mahvish came to my room, and we chatted before my radiation oncologist came in. I narrated how I had discovered the lump and what treatment was decided for me. Mahvish wears her feelings on her face. I could see her distress as she listened on. I knew this woman had a heart of gold. She then wrote down her phone number and said, "Niyati, contact me for anything you need, anything at all."

And thus started a friendship in the unlikeliest of circumstances. Now whenever I have my follow-ups at the cancer center, I message Mahvish. More often than not, she comes out to see me . . . we hug, we laugh, we reminisce.

When you're far from home, having roots in the Indian subcontinent is a uniting factor—not dividing. (The Indian subcontinent comprises India, Pakistan, Nepal, Bangladesh, Sri Lanka, and the Maldives.)

What I have given you here are chronological snippets of self-discovery. I have learned much about myself by moving countries. The experience of living on three different continents has presented me with the opportunity to venture, fumble, learn, and improve. I hope this journey lasts a lifetime.

Nuwan and I often talk about "where to next?" We want to provide similar opportunities for self-discovery for our half-Indian, half-Lankan, American-born kids.

10. SCHOOLING THEN AND NOW

"I'm not concerned about your comfort zone or readiness for change. I'm concerned about the kids who just entered kindergarten."
— Ian Jukes

The fabric of my being is enriched by the embroidery of ancient threads representing my forefathers' quest for a better life. This tapestry contains rich colors of my ethnicity, the Indian culture that I revere deeply and challenge in equal parts. My immigrant story weaves it all together on the canvas of education. You already know how much I value education from the stories I so proudly tell about my lineage. It should then be no surprise that I include a chapter on the school system.

In India, most parents from the lower-middle class and above send their children to private schools. Public schools are available but have large class sizes and teachers who are underqualified and underpaid. My sister and I went to private school. When we lived in the suburbs, I went to Jamnabai Narsee, a school that is home to many celebrity children. I acknowledge that I had an advantaged upbringing, and the schools I attended were elite.

In that setting, I want to point out that my kindergarten class size was fifty-some children. That is the situation in a private school that is home to celebrity kids; now consider that the state-run public schools are two or three times that size. Private school also provides the best chance at getting an English education, putting private school children at an advantage over public schoolers.

Getting into a reputable private school in a densely populated city like Mumbai is fiercely competitive. There's an application process, an application fee, and sometimes a suggested "donation" to get one foot in the door. On the application form, parents are asked soul-searching questions. Once your application is accepted, both the parents and the child are invited for an interview. After the adults exchange pleasantries, a one-on-one interview occurs with the aspiring kindergartener. If the five-year-old passes the interview and you have the financial means to afford the tuition, you might get into the private school. Some parents opt to enroll their toddlers in interview-coaching classes to prepare the child for the questioning.

It's tough. But maybe that's what makes us resilient. I wish it weren't so, though. There is something precious about being able to preserve a child's innocence—about not needing to send a toddler to interview-etiquette class.

In the U.S., like in India, there is an undeniable right to free education. Public schools in the U.S. are funded by federal, state, and local tax dollars. Higher quality schools are usually accompanied by higher property taxes. Low-income neighborhoods are at a disadvantage due to this disparity.

Nuwan and I feel the school district we live in now will provide the necessary resources for our children to succeed. So, we decided to enroll Vihaan in public kindergarten. Since neither of us did our primary school education here in the U.S., the system was new to us. The enrollment process was, for lack of a better phrase, as easy as ABC. I went to Richard's Elementary School, filled out a form, provided proof of our address and Vihaan's immunization record. The form didn't even need a passport-sized photo of Vihaan. That was it; my child was enrolled in school.

When I called my mother to tell her this, she asked, "What about the admission fees?" I told her there weren't any. I informed her that the school provides textbooks and worksheets at no direct cost to the parent. There is a school supply list that we needed to furnish—markers, crayons, folders, etc. The school also provides subsidized or free meals to all students. We send Vihaan his lunch and a snack, but I know there is an option for him to use the school cafeteria—which we might do later, when he is older.

Something else covered by the state and our taxes is transportation. The iconic yellow school bus comes to most neighborhoods that are greater than two miles away from school. Fun fact: Vihaan's school bus driver is a woman! Another fun fact: there is a seat for every child, and the bus driver waits for the child to be seated and assists with any seat belt needs before taking off. Kids these days have no idea how much life caters to them!

When I rode the school bus, I was lucky if I could find an empty seat. By the time I was in fifth grade, I remedied that situation. I figured out the public transportation system. The public bus depot was right by my apartment complex, which meant buses started their route there. Boarding the bus at its first stop guaranteed me a seat. The cost of riding the bus was 50 *paise* for a half-ticket. Children under sixteen were considered half-ticket, half the cost of an adult. It would be like a child here needing a dime; it wasn't a lot of money. I was given money for snacks at the cafeteria, so 50 *paise* was what I took from my snack money.

Unbeknownst to my mother, I created a new school routine for myself.

Morning ride on the public bus, afternoon return on the school bus . . . till my bubble burst. She saw me one morning at the public bus stop in my white school uniform, big glasses, and a backpack twice my size. My mother pulled over and said, "Niyati? What are you doing here?!" The jig was up.

I hopped into her car and sheepishly told her, "It's nice that I don't have to stand the whole way with my heavy school bag." To appear smart, I added, "Also, *Aai*, I don't need to wait till the bus stops at the bus stop. There's a traffic light close to school. I wait right by the exit, and if the light is red, I hop out and walk to school." (*Aai* is mother in Marathi.)

What does an Indian mother say to her pre-teen using public transportation and hopping off at a light? "I'm paying through my nose for the school bus, and you're not riding it?! From now on, you can take the public bus back as well." Quarterly school bus fees were about four times the cost of riding public transportation. Then again, the city bus was not designed for children to ride without an accompanying adult. How many ten-year-olds in school uniforms have you seen riding the New York subway by themselves?

Disclaimer: In the past three decades, things have changed a lot in Mumbai. My nephew rides the school bus, and every child has a seat on the bus.

Vihaan's bussing experience so far has been a touch different. One day when my son was in line to take the bus back home, he realized he had forgotten his superhero water bottle in his classroom. The bus line progressed, and Vihaan started crying. The principal of the elementary school, Mr. Sprong, noticed the waterworks and asked, "What's wrong, buddy?" A teary-eyed Vihaan told him about his bottle. Mr. Sprong offered some words of encouragement and let the bus driver know that there would be a distraught kid on board. He then let Vihaan's kindergarten teacher, Mrs. Park, know about the crisis. When the bus pulled into our neighborhood, I picked up a very upset kindergartener. To calm Vihaan down, I suggested, "We can text Mrs. Park and ask her to keep the bottle safe in class for you."

Before I go on with this riveting, missing bottle story that *I know* has you on the edge of your seat, I want to acknowledge something. I am surrounded by kind souls who make themselves reachable to my frantic soul: my oncologists and several nurses from the cancer center, all of whom I tap on periodically. Executives who walk the path of empathy and want to support me, including the company officers who are so high up on the totem pole that I am a mere blade of grass from their vantage point. But most important of all these connections is the underappreciated kindergarten teacher who shares her personal cell phone number— to a phone that is not sponsored by the school district—to be there for a six-year-old.

Back to my story: Mrs. Park responded to my text saying that she'd heard. She then asked if she could talk to Vihaan over the phone. I was touched and thankful she wanted to address this minor *crisis* in my son's life. I put her on speaker phone.

"Vihaan, this is Mrs. Park. I found your water bottle, and I've kept it safe for you on your table."

After some head nodding and deep breaths, as per Mrs. Park's instructions over the phone, Vihaan calmed down.

This trivial incident made Nuwan and me both comment on how involved the elementary school principal was! In the bus line, Mr. Sprong had made an effort to tell the teacher that a student was upset—*over a water bottle*. You know, a pretty big deal in a kindergartener's life.

Growing up in India, my school principal walked on water, further emboldened by the fact that she was a nun. I don't recall any overt acts of compassion. Heck, I lost my father at thirteen, and the principal didn't so much as talk to me. Her act of kindness was that since I missed my midterm exams—you know, with the broken bones, concussion, dead dad and all—I was permitted to take (not *re-take*, but *take*!) it a few weeks later. I admit I'm comparing 1990s Mumbai and the 2020 Midwest, which is not entirely fair. But this is the contrast I see in our upbringing.

Strict schooling in an all-girls' Catholic school has two priorities: one, to provide an exceptional English-language education, and two, to ensure that we act like young ladies.

I remember getting trained on how to "sit like a lady," "act like a lady," and "cross your legs." I had a lot of energy as a child, and these conformity lessons fell on deaf ears. I liked to play and run around. Much to the chagrin of my school administration, I had the audacity to be a child. While I was good at using my spider-senses to know when the nuns were around, there was one time I got caught running during recess. *The sacrilege!* The principal grabbed me by the arm and hit me in the back, as she reprimanded me for "not acting like a lady." I was stunned. My parents never spanked us. *What gave this adult the right to raise her hand at me?* I was little, but I knew my rights.

When I got home from school, I waited till my mother came home, and as soon as she walked through the door, I started crying. "Sister Gloria hit me," I told her, almost as if I were outing a serious criminal. My mother consoled me, reassuring me, "We should talk to Baba when he's back."

My father came home a few hours later. I showed him my back and told him I was punished—struck—for running during recess. I don't think I've ever seen my father that angry. He was fuming. His body language screamed: *no one raises a hand on my children!* He was silent through dinner—furious, but silent—and said he would take me to school the next morning.

The next morning, Baba took me to school, parked his car, and walked in with me—something parents weren't supposed to do unless they had an appointment with the principal. He went straight to the principal's office, while telling me, "Wait outside."

I don't know what he said to Sister Gloria; I was afraid to eavesdrop. But when he left, Sister Gloria came up to me and said, "Niyati, I think we had a *misunderstanding*." No formal apology, but this is the closest and most dramatic acceptance of fault I had witnessed from a nun.

••

While this might seem inconsequential—a tiny spanking—I debate what message we send our children when we spank them. From infancy, children learn by imitating. They mimic facial expressions, learn how to sit and walk, adopt language by imitating sounds. What does a child learn when their caregiver uses corporal punishment instead of talking and reason to mitigate a situation? For me, it demonstrates that if a person of authority is physically larger than the receiver, violence is acceptable—and physical violence can be used to correct behavior.

A year or so ago, I was enjoying a work lunch with an eclectic group of employees: Indians from India, and ones that grew up in the Middle East; Africans from Nigeria and Ivory Coast; and African Americans from the Midwest. We were talking about school and the tactics used to discipline rowdy kids. I talked about the go-to punishment rendered by my teachers when we were disorderly. We girls were made to kneel on gravel for about an hour, in the peak of the afternoon, under the scorching hot sun—without water breaks.

Before I could create drama, a few of my colleagues started chuckling, saying, "You call that punishment?" Then one after another, they started sharing their childhood experiences. The stories started small—of teachers using a ruler on the palm. I thought, *that was brutal; no one ever hit me with a ruler.* Some of my lunch-mates talked about the use of a stick. *Alright, that's ridiculous; what teacher had the freedom to spank at will with whatever weapon was available?* My Nigerian colleagues told me about how their teachers handled punishment. When a disobedient kid needed punishing, the teacher would pick another student to administer the punishment. If the chosen one did not administer the spanking with vigor and enthusiasm, the teacher would give them both a walloping. I can't think of the psychological damage this practice does to the child getting beaten by his cohort—*and* the child who was asked to be cruel.

But that day at lunch, we were all laughing in stupefaction as we shared anecdotes. Humor—there must be a reason why evolution didn't weed it out. Humor can act like a pressure relief valve, and that day at lunch, we were all using humor to laugh off practices that I deem fundamentally wrong.

I understand this is a generational and regional thing, and it all depends on where you grew up and in what decade. But under any circumstance, I don't agree with striking a child. What irks me most is when parents say a child is "too old to spank." I feel that implies one of two things: the child is an adult, and striking an adult is felony assault or battery (yes, I watch my crime shows intently); or the child you want to spank is now six inches taller and outweighs you, too, so if they hit back, you are toast. I reckon *too old to spank* is about the parent realizing they don't have the stronger hand anymore. It hardly seems to be about the child.

I understand this is a polarizing topic. I seek rationalization but don't buy any of the excuses for corporal punishment. I am thankful that my parents didn't resort to physical violence as form of corrective action. Look how well I turned out (big eyes and coy smile)!

•••

I would like to argue, if sports were a bigger part of my schooling, I wouldn't have as much pent-up energy—and likely wouldn't have gotten in trouble as often. Getting in trouble for running during recess—yes, I was a nonconformist. Wait, I *am* a nonconformist. Sports and education are intimately connected.

There is disparity between college sports in the U.S. versus Asia or England. In Indo-Lanka, college sports are almost non-existent. Even when they exist, they are not your ticket to free tuition, scholarships, or financial freedom. Back home in India, the purpose of college is to get a degree, not to kick a ball around. Imagine two circles: one is sporting, and the other is a college education. And the two circles don't intersect. Sports and education are mutually exclusive.

From my limited knowledge, college athletics have some relevance in the U.K., but even there, disparity exists. While being selected for the rowing team at Oxford or Cambridge is rather prestigious, it wasn't till the turn of the century that Cambridge launched an athletic scholarship program.

Enter the United States of America; being an exceptional athlete at the high school level might very well be your ticket to a free ride. You haven't seen college sports till you experience American college football. My bias is the league my alma mater belongs to—the Big Ten. To quote a line about Ohio State football from a frame Nuwan made for me when we were dating, "Big spirit, big wins, big money." That big spirit translates to college pride—and college branded clothing and accessories. Nuwan once told me how strange he found it that someone fifty years out of college still sports a "Go Bucks" hoodie. Nuwan didn't fully realize the impact of college sports. For example, college football is televised, commercialized, and a disproportionately huge money maker for the university. As a result, stakeholders continue pumping money into college football, recruit the top high school graduates to be players, sell tickets at premium cost, fill up a stadium full of screaming football fanatics, make money on merchandise, and repeat the cycle year in and year out. These stadiums I talk about, they are staggering. To illustrate my point, if you Google the largest stadiums by capacity for any sport across the globe, you will find three Big Ten schools in the top five largest capacity stadiums in the world. Go ahead, Google it.

Capacity translates to mania and money.

I have wondered if Indian colleges could adopt the American football fever by channeling the Indian fervor for—drumroll—cricket! Picture this: regional colleges form conferences with cool names like *Bade Miyan, Hum Majbut* . . . I could go on. To my non-Hindi speaking readers, I'm just making a parody of a popular Bollywood movie, and the other is a cheesy phrase. We could have regional conferences, teams, and mascots—and a dedicated cricket season, preferably in the cooler winter months rather than the monsoon or summer season. Might be a nifty way to raise funds for the school.

•••

Our time in the Fall of 2020 was preoccupied with things bigger than college ball: youth soccer! We signed Vihaan up for an eight-week soccer program. He was on a coed team of five- and six-year-olds called the Pathfinders. At their first practice game, the kids were given orange T-shirts as their uniform, each with their name on the back. It was so cute. The coaches were two fathers who volunteered to coach the aspiring soccer stars. This was our first taste of sports leagues and organized events for children.

Vihaan's opening soccer match was a right spectacle. The set of soccer fields that hosted all of the games was a group of thirty fields of different sizes. Not all are full-sized; there are smaller fields for the young children. The parking lot was bursting at its seams. Tens of cars, dare I say close to a hundred cars, dotted around any safe space for parking. We found a spot, rather far away from the field. As we walked toward our designated field, I couldn't help but gape. Streams of parents, grandparents, children in soccer jerseys, siblings, and babies hauled across by the parents. It was a sight to take in.

Vihaan united with his team, and they played their first match against the green team.

I wish I could say I was a cool, unconcerned parent on the sidelines swiping at my phone. But sadly, I was the impassioned mother screaming at Vihaan, words of encouragement of course, "Eye on the ball! Turn it around [something I said often when Vihaan was kicking toward the wrong side]! Get in there, Vihaan! Pay attention!!" I laugh now, but it was intense. An insider has cautioned me that there are videos on how not to be a bad soccer parent. It is all about how not to ruin the game by being too competitive on the sidelines.

As much as I yelled, my applause for the *both* teams on the field was just as gregarious. Youth soccer is amazing. I never knew where the forty minutes went, but it ended with happy tots who were given a healthy snack and something to drink.

This might seem run-of-the-mill for Americans, but you don't understand how impressive it was for an immigrant like me. I had seen nothing like it. For those eight weeks, the practice and game-Saturdays were my highlight. A highlight for all of us, really. The streams of cars rolling in, squeals of children, proud parents clapping and cheering, some tears from the little ones especially when they got hit by the ball—but smiles at the end. I was hooked.

Something that has bothered me in the past reared its ugly head: why is it that even in elementary level sports, the players are assigned uniforms, but students are not required to wear a uniform in school? I'll be honest, I hated my school uniform growing up. I wore a white blouse and white skirt, paired with white socks and black leather flats. It was so hard to keep the white pristine. On the days we had physical education, we needed to wear white canvas shoes, the bane of my existence. If keeping a white uniform spotless was hard, the canvas shoes would turn into a brown, muddy mess after PE. The mandate was that we must wash our canvas shoes weekly, and once dry, use white paint or whitener to coat the shoes and laces to restore them to their brilliant white. This was just *mental*; why wear white shoes for sports?

The only color in our uniforms was a little badge we wore with the school name and color of the "house" we belonged to. In India, following the British education system, students were divided into four or five houses—which are groups within the school—which compete against each other. The competitions might be in elocution, sports, debates, posters, and more.

My school, St. Anne's, split us into four houses. St. Matthew was represented by a red color; St. John, green; St. Luke, yellow; and St. Mark, blue. I was part of St. John, so I wore a tiny green badge, and that was my spot of color in my uniform. We would refer to the student body at assembly as "Matthew-Mark-Luke-John, take your places."

I asked Nuwan if they followed the house system in Sri Lanka. Of course, they did, but their school used more traditional representation: *Shoor*, *Veer*—which are two words for brave in Sanskrit; *Meththa*—which means kind; and *Shanta*—which is peace. I heard schools in the U.S. didn't divide children up into houses; *how in the world do you have elocution competitions?*

Anyhow, back to my blah uniform. We were only allowed gold studs for earrings, our hair had to be braided if long, a ponytail was accepted for short hair, unruly hair must be pinned back with a black hairband, and the hair ties needed to be black. If we chose to wear a watch, it needed to be—no points for guessing the color—yes, black! We weren't allowed to paint our nails either.

My favorite thing to do at the start of summer or Diwali holiday (Hindu festival of lights) was to paint my nails. I felt like such a rebel. Of course, we would acetone-scrub our nails clean before returning to school. I hope it's abundantly obvious that makeup of any sort was not allowed. If your Chapstick glistened like lip gloss, you would be in trouble. In the winter months though, we were allowed a bright red sweater. I loved winter days just for the added color to my uniform.

I hated how strict schools were on uniform policy and grooming. But now that I look back, I realize how lucky we were. A school uniform is a great equalizer for children. The strict "no-bling" policy meant there was little opportunity to show off. Of course, we knew who the rich kids were—they showed up in fancy cars—but in class, we were equals. No fancy earrings or diamonds, only a plain jane watch, and a uniform purchased from one of two stores in town literally meant *we all looked alike*.

The uniform also differentiated us from the teachers. They wore regular clothes, while we were a sea of white. This contrast reminded us of our place—as students.

Another thing I realized when I spent a winter with my cousins who were in high school (without a dress code) was the amount of thought and effort that went into deciding what to wear to school the next day. I admit, I spent futile hours cleaning my canvas shoes when I could have been doing something more fun, but there was a beauty in the monotony. Choosing outfits, matching earrings, deciding on flats or boots and which type of socks—it all seems like a massive effort in vanity. I'm also going to guess that this exercise has a greater (negative) impact on girls than it does on high school boys. So, I circle back to my question, if we use a uniformed

T-shirt to play kindergarten-level sports, why not apply the same simple equalizer in the classroom?

While you ponder that question, I am reminded that this is just the start. Nuwan and I will learn much more about school and the education system here as Vihaan and Aarini grow up.

All I can say is that when we get to prom age, I'll have to write another book on Nuwan. He is not ready for that. (And I'm probably not either.)

11. INSATIABLE

> "Hinduism comes closest to being a nature religion. Rivers, rocks, trees, plants, animals, and birds all play their part, both in mythology and everyday worship."
> —*Ruskin Bond,* Rain in the Mountains: Notes from the Himalayas

Someone famous once said that *the cure for boredom is curiosity, and there is no cure for curiosity.* I love it; hear me out—curiosity is a chronic condition! If there's one trait I've had since childhood and continue to hold true to my heart, it is curiosity. I think engineers and scientists are intrinsically curious. The desire to invent and innovate, the striving to understand the human body and brain, a voracious appetite for exploring the world and seeing what is outside our planet; all this stems from curiosity. *What is out there? What is inside of us? What are we made of?*

My fascination with the cosmos started with a simple revelation about the sun. At St. Anne's School, we had library period once a week. I was always drawn to books on the solar system and the universe in general. One library period, I picked up a book on stars. The first chapter was about the sun. I skimmed through; *yes, yes, sun, the brilliant star—I know all this.* And then I read something that could not have been true. The book said that our solar system orbits around the Milky Way galaxy. *What?* We were taught that the sun is a star, and stars are stationary objects. Planets revolve around the star. The book contradicted that. I was baffled. Were our textbooks inaccurate, or was the inconsistency intentional, because the school board assumed children lack the intellectual capacity to grasp that just as the planets revolve around the sun, the solar system revolves around the galaxy? I knew better than to question the authority of our totalitarian teachers, but I whispered to myself, "The sun is not stationary."

I wanted to learn *everything* they were keeping from us. When you're eleven, you can make such statements as, "I will learn everything."

I think about children today and how deluded we parents must be to think that we can hide anything from their young, bright, resourceful minds. And no, I don't mean astrophysics. I mean the hard truth, the tough topics, things we want to shield our children from, but they know better. That is the big divide between our parents' generation and our own. The access to information, internet, and libraries the size of town halls breeds more confidence to talk to an adult—or even question one.

As for me, it was simple. I needed to rid myself of ignorance and misinformation by reading. So, after visiting my school library and having the world opened up to me, I went on a quest to learn about the truths of the universe. I read about supernovas, white dwarfs and the eventual demise of the sun and black holes. The whole time I was thinking, *there is a bottomless well of information; does everyone know this?* It was a revelation.

But I was too scared to spread the rumor that there was more knowledge in books than our supreme teachers knew.

At the age of fourteen, I picked up *A Brief History of Time* by Stephen Hawking. I did not completely understand it, but I read it, took notes, and asked my older friends to explain quantum physics to me. If the library book on stars was an eye-opener for me, the Hawking book was a game changer. I would spend more time studying that book than doing schoolwork. What fueled my desire to learn wasn't physics or math; it was curiosity, and that curiosity was insatiable.

A few years later, when I was seventeen, the national news and local newspapers reported that Stephen Hawking was going to be in India in January 2001! He would be giving a lecture at an international physics seminar at the Tata Institute of Fundamental Research (TIFR) in Mumbai. My hero was going to be in my city. My mother basically moved mountains to get me a student ticket to the talk. The ticket she got was for second row, right behind Mr. Hawking's wife. Less than a year away from reaching adulthood and moving countries, I watched my hero talk about his life and success against all odds. At the end of the talk, I spoke to Mr. Hawking's wife and extended my hand to shake hers.

When you have that experience as a teenager, life can only build on it. Still recovering from Hawking-fever, I declared my major at Ohio State to be astrophysics, something I later changed to electrical and computer engineering purely for job prospects upon graduation.

My mother worked tirelessly to spark and aid my curiosity—and continues to do so. She encourages me to pursue a path less traveled. I am lucky to have a mother who fought so fiercely to provide opportunities that bolstered my courage.

•••

My affair with the heavens continued. While I was an undergraduate engineering student—you know, the time I went with my schoolmates to Texas and was pulled over by border patrol?—I got a chance to see the night sky like never before. The four of us hiked a few miles from our tents, found a quiet spot, huddled under blankets, and stared into the sky.

We were not avid stargazers, yet there was pin drop silence that echoed our surroundings. I laid on the blanket to absorb the vastness of the sky, which was only interrupted by the horizon. I realized at that moment that humanity has spent its entirety claiming nature, owning it and taming it. But here under a blanket of stars, the universe is telling me, *I don't play by your rules.*

One doesn't need be an astronomer to look up at the heavens and have an existential awakening. The stillness of that night, the silence that spoke to my soul, and the vastness of the heavens made it clear to me that I am but a blip. I decided right then, *I must seek this tranquility*. This became my lifelong spiritual journey.

The second half of our road trip was to North Padre island, a serene beach that allows only camping; there are no structures or hotels there. The four of us set up our tents and started a little fire to warm our toes. Andrea interrupted, "Make a wish; there is a shooting star." We all looked up, and over a matter of minutes, we saw several shooting stars. I saw one with a slight comet's tail as it burned into the atmosphere. Seeing shooting stars felt like it was a blessing from . . . well, from whatever you believe in.

The next morning, the park ranger told us that it was a meteor shower.

•••

I kept on my journey; I did not become an astrophysicist, but I harnessed my inquisitiveness for the cosmos. It was 2008, and I was three years into a full-time job as an engineer. It offered good pay, and I had no dependents I needed to care for. So that summer, I coordinated a trip with eight other friends from Wisconsin, Illinois, Canada, South Korea, and Japan to engage in the four-day hike to Machu Picchu in Peru. The hike starts at 10,000 feet above sea level in Cusco, transcends to 14,000 feet above sea level, then descends on the ruins of Machu Picchu on day four.

I was advised before the hike to look for the Milky Way, and that it would be a journey in self-realization. I wondered: *how will I know I'm looking at the Milky Way?*

Day two of the hike, after we conquered Dead Woman's Pass at 14,000 feet, we got to base camp—exhausted. I trekked the tail end of that hike in darkness, with a head lamp strapped to my forehead. That night, the group ate vegetarian quinoa soup and eggplant; it was the type of tummy comfort the body needed after a high-altitude, tough hike.

The night was dark with no moon in the sky. As I walked out of our dinner tent to my individual tent for the night, I looked up at the sky. And there it was! Maybe it was my fatigue or being at high altitude, maybe it was the scarcity of oxygen at those elevations, but I slow-motion dropped to my knees. No explanation needed, the Milky Way Galaxy was looking down on me, and I was star-struck (pun intended). *This is OUR galaxy. I see it now; I bow in gratitude.*

The Milky Way presented itself as a thick cloud made up of millions of stars; the brightness of the cloud was unmistakable. Goodness, if I could dish out one piece of advice, go see the Milky Way—in Utah or Alaska—or better yet go see it from the southern hemisphere. It had a profound impact on me. To know I am but a spot in the history of human civilization, to realize the insignificance of my cosmological existence, is a humbling exercise and one we should all practice.

•••

Hawking, meteors, the Milky Way . . . I continue to build my astro-nerd, wannabe cosmo-nut resume.

It was our second wedding anniversary, and I wanted to surprise my better half with a holiday in the Arctic Circle. Because nothing says romance more than taking your spouse to northern Finland in the peak of winter. This ridiculous trip to Finland had only one agenda—to experience the aurora borealis. I wanted to see the Northern Lights in their splendor, away from light pollution and in a region where a display is almost guaranteed if it is a clear night.

We flew from London to Helsinki and then on a puddle jumper to Kittila Airport. We were officially in the Arctic Circle, in the middle of nowhere, in the northwestern part of Finland close to the border of Sweden—*in the freaking tundra*. We picked up our backpacks and went to the exit of the airport, looking for our ride to from Kittila Airport to Akaslampolo, which is where we were planning on staying in a log cabin.

Our driver showed up in a sweatshirt, no hat, no jacket, no gloves, and flip-flops. *Open- toed shoes in Scandinavian winter.* The roads we drove on, with chains on the tires, were buried under a few feet of thick ice. There was no actual road to be seen. And the trees alongside the road were eerie impersonations of ancient men. Big arms, drooping shoulders, heads sloped, the trees looked like they were going to start walking toward us like in a zombie apocalypse movie.

During the first few days, we went to a reindeer farm, did some husky dogsledding, and went snowmobiling. Each night, we went on an excursion with a ranger in the woods looking for the aurora. But no dice.

For the last night, I had us booked in a fancy, igloo-shaped hotel room, where the igloo dome was made of glass. This clear roof provided staggering views of the Lappish countryside: snow-covered trees, vast landscapes, and uninterrupted views of the sky. It would be a dreamy place to see the Northern Lights from the warmth and comfort of our bed, as we lay gazing up at the sky.

This was our last opportunity to see the aurora. Fortunately, it was a clear night, so our chances seemed good. Almost as if our excitement were palpable to the cosmos, the sun decided to put on a spectacular show for us. The display started with doubt, as Nuwan tentatively said, "I think I see the northern lights." In disbelief, I ran closer to the window dome of our igloo pod and thought I saw a green shadow, too. *It can't be.* Not fully convinced, we put on our many layers of winter clothing and went outside to observe the sky without a shield of glass. I was afraid the glass was playing tricks on my vision.

I saw a cloud hovering in the sky. It had that iconic, characteristic green that I've seen in photographs of the aurora borealis. A few seconds later, the cloud swerved a little—and then moved dramatically. I was ecstatic. These clouds moved in a way that no cloud moves. It was swift, erratic, and seemingly unnatural.

In a matter of seconds, the spooky green cloud disappeared. After a moment of silence, another green blob suddenly appeared out of nowhere. It, too, performed a dance routine and ended with a disappearing act. The indistinct clouds turned into defined streaks; the dance of lights became more enticing as the night proceeded.

Nuwan took photographs on his tripod. A little past midnight, we retired into our igloo, because I was freezing. Inside, I was finally able to feel my fingertips and toes again. My face was burning hot from the extreme temperature shift. With so much excitement and adrenaline pumping through my system, there was no way either of us would be able to sleep. Nuwan was in and out of the room taking pictures. The bed was designed for aurora viewings, so it was adjustable. I raised the bed and positioned myself so I could continue looking at the Northern Lights all night.

As the night progressed, the aurora became even more impressive. The ballet got more elaborate, and each time a new dancer (streak) appeared, a larger portion of the sky was enveloped. There were times when I saw two streaks approach each other from either side of the sky, collide, form a big blob in the center, spiral around like a galaxy, and disperse. There was one point—and only one point in the night, around 1:30 a.m.—when the entire night sky was consumed by the aurora borealis. I saw spirals right above my head, streaks in the horizon, and splotches in the middle. It was an inexplicable cosmic encounter and hard to comprehend that something this extraordinary could be visible from Earth.

Nuwan and I drifted in and out of sleep, not wanting to miss the celestial drama. After eluding us for four straight nights, finally on our last night of the holiday, we experienced the Northern Lights in all their glory. If it was even possible, I have a greater appreciation and total respect for Mother Earth and the extraordinary world out there.

•••

Why stop here, when each experience enriches my appreciation of the universe? On August 21, 2017, the United States was in for a cosmic treat. A total solar eclipse would be visible across the U.S., from the Pacific coast in Oregon to the Atlantic coast in South Carolina.

Nuwan and I drove to Hopkinsville, Kentucky, with two other friends, Pallav and Mayura, to witness this phenomenon. It was us and about 100,000 other visitors who descended upon "Eclipseville." The interstate and smaller state routes linking civilization to Hopkinsville had a line of hundreds of cars all heading one way—to the epicenter of the eclipse. It was like a scene out of an Armageddon movie.

The eclipse started around noon. We looked up at the sun with our solar-eclipse glasses and saw in amazement as a tiny part of the sun had been bitten off at the one o'clock position. It was unnatural to see a blotch on the brilliant sun. That little notch of darkness kept growing, as if the sun were being swallowed by a dragon. Over the course of an hour and a half, strange things happened as the sun got progressively more eclipsed and only a small glowing crescent remained. Daylight turned into an inexplicable twilight. It was not the kind of darkness you experience in the evenings—but a subdued light, almost as if the environment around us had a photo-filter. It went from scorching 90-degree heat, to a slightly cooler feel. Cicadas started chirping, and the critters got louder as it got darker. It was remarkable that even at 99 percent eclipse, the sun's powerful rays still lit up the Earth. Above us was the night sky with stars, and around us the horizon had this subtle orange glow. It did not feel like dawn or dusk; it was neither day nor night. It was like nothing I had experienced before, and nothing could prepare me for it.

We saw the last bits of sunlight pass through the moon's valleys, and for a solid two minutes and forty seconds, we experienced totality. We could see the sun's atmosphere and the exquisite solar flares with our naked eyes! It was a life-changing experience. I don't know how else to describe how absolutely insane it was to be able to see solar flares from here on Earth.

Totality ended abruptly, as the blinding diamond ring appeared. The diamond ring is said to be 400,000 times brighter than the sun's corona and not safe to view without eye protection. We had to put our glasses back on, and that was it; the corona was no longer visible. Those were the fastest two minutes and forty seconds of my life. Nuwan and I checked our watches to see where the time went. We were convinced that there must have been a disruption in the space-time continuum, because it felt like no longer than a few seconds.

The moon's shadow, or umbra, traveled through Kentucky at a staggering 1,462 miles per hour. After this first solar eclipse experience, I am now a self-proclaimed *umbraphile* (NPR taught me this word; it means "shadow lover" and is used to describe eclipse chasers). I was surprised when I read that no other planet in our solar system experiences a total solar eclipse.

For all the control we think we have, the dams and levees we build, the storms we prepare for and tides we predict, here is our cratered moon giving us a glimpse of the sun's magnificence.

Totality for some is a spiritual experience, and for others, it is the hand of God. Not only are we blessed to be on this planet, but also, we are conscious beings who have the intelligence to understand and appreciate the movement of celestial objects.

I can see how some might not feel the same amount of enthusiasm about the heavens, and that dropping to your knees when you witness the Milky Way for the first time might seem a touch dramatic. I hear you. But my little life would be lackluster without this unbridled amazement and insatiable curiosity. I feel: *if I don't know the bigger picture, how will I ever know my place in the universe?*

A fundamental question that has plagued humankind for ages is, "What's the meaning of life?" In *Unafraid*, I talked about the purpose of life, when my neighbor Ghalila told me her purpose in that moment was to provide meals for me as I went through cancer treatment. It was not profound, but it was extraordinarily impactful.

The meaning of life, however, is much harder to answer, and no one has answered it to my satisfaction; not the sadhus and yogis or theologians, not even scientists whom I respect so much. To understand the meaning of life, we should have some idea of our cosmological significance. It's about knowing our place in the grand*est* scheme. Some claim we are lead actors in a movie called life. I counter; there is a cosmic production of epic proportions, and we are here for its validation. God has given us relentless curiosity, the intellectual capacity to explore and question, the ability to understand and appreciate. I bow to the cosmos. Humbled by its grandeur, my spiritual journey continues, and I am reminded of my place in the universe—tiny but not insignificant.

12. THE PANDEMIC

"Love and compassion are necessities, not luxuries.
Without them, humanity cannot survive."
—*Dalai Lama XIV, The Art of Happiness*

From being in love with and fascinated by Mother Nature, I am reminded of her wrath. Have you seen the 2011 movie called *Contagion*? You must watch it. It's star-studded with the Damons and Winslets of Hollywood. Bonus, it's even got Morpheus and Walter White! But watch it for the storyline. The movie is about a highly contagious respiratory virus that originated in the Far East but rapidly spread all over the world, causing a pandemic. It is unnerving because that movie plays a lot like our reality in 2020.

It was the beginning of 2020 when the world first heard about a new flu-like virus that originated in Wuhan, China. An American returning to the States from Wuhan brought this virus to North America. Around the same time, the virus spread to nearby Japan, Thailand, and South Korea. But it wasn't yet a cause of international alarm. China was quick to cordon off Wuhan, canceling all flights and trains into the area and suspending public transportation.

My teammate lives and works in Wuhan. We would ask him about the situation every week. I was concerned for him and his family, but not panicked. *I'm sure they will isolate the virus soon, and life will go back to normal.*

By the end of the month, the World Health Organization (WHO) declared a global health emergency, and the United States suspended foreign nationals from entering the U.S. if they had traveled to China. I was baffled that the WHO would declare a global emergency when the virus didn't even have a name. It wasn't till February that a name was devised. Novel **co**rona **vi**rus **d**isease 20**19** was dubbed as COVID-19. Europe started seeing cases, and Italy became the new epicenter of this virus. The unprecedented rise in Italy's death toll had everyone speculating. Entire towns were in lockdown. The word *pandemic* started getting used to describe the health crisis.

My immediate worry was for India. We are neighbors with China; how will India contain the spread with our high population density?

Health experts the world over started instructing people to wear face masks and wash hands thoroughly. India was quick to adopt that practice, and local news channels broadcast the safety precautions and implemented travel restrictions. Nuwan predicted early on that hand sanitizer and face masks would be in short supply. He was spot on. Furthermore, there were no disinfectant wipes or sanitizer bottles to be found. The internet was boasting recipes for making your own alcohol-based sanitizer at home. Savvy men and women took to the sewing machines to make cloth masks. Some gave them away at no cost; others charged a premium.

India went into one of the strictest lockdowns seen by any country in the world, and the citizens obeyed.

Face masks, social distancing, sanitizing, and six-foot distance when queuing became the new protocol everywhere. What ensued in the early months of 2020 was reminiscent of a dark period in human history: the 1918 Spanish flu. The Spanish flu infected nearly a third of the world's population and wiped out some 50 million people. COVID-19 was trending that way.

By the middle of March 2020, coronavirus cases started to appear in our small town of Columbus. We decided to pull the kids out of daycare, even though daycare had a new screening process in place for temperature, symptoms and recent contact with any COVID-positive person. I stopped going into the office like many others the world over, assuming a work-from-home lifestyle. Eventually, Nuwan stopped going to the office as well, when our company sent out a bulletin urging only "essential workers" to step into the office.

Essential workers—now that is a sobering and eye-opening phrase. Before the pandemic, I thought I knew who constituted essential workers. Doctors, nurses, emergency room technicians—basically health care workers. When we got our remote work bulletin, that's when I truly understood the phrase. Our production line was to remain open; our manufacturing workers were asked to come in. Most of the test cells, a validation area where engines are tested, remained open. Cleaning staff and janitorial work became even more important for overall hygiene and to stop the spread—they were essential. Grocery stores needed to remain open, and pharmacies. They were essential, as were gas stations. Managers, CEOs, and consultants could almost all do their jobs from home. It was the hands-on work that was essential. This realization was humbling.

With growing uncertainty came fear. Death tolls all over the world were rising rapidly. But with this also came the unmissable abundance of generosity. Greatness from people in all walks of life epitomized empathy and compassion. I write some of the stories here so that in the years and decades to come, when we talk about the COVID-19 pandemic, we don't lose sight of the acts of heroism.

I'd like to start this with the story of a centenarian and a WWII veteran, Captain Tom Moore. It was Captain Tom's hundredth birthday, at what seemed to be the height of the pandemic. The captain wanted to make his hundredth memorable by raising $1,000 for the U.K.'s National Health Service (NHS) charities, since they had helped him during his cancer treatment and when he had a broken hip. His brilliant plan to raise funds was a pledge to walk one hundred laps around his back garden before the big 1-0-0th birthday, with the assistance of a walker. There's an image of him on a treadmill at home preparing for this self-imposed challenge. A popular fundraising site was used and the goal set to $1,000. Within the first hour of his lap-taking, Captain Tom raised $70,000!

News outlets featured his story, and it went viral. Celebrities—Formula One champions, cricketers, snooker champions, world-famous violinists, and famous actors sent out congratulatory videos, all thanking him for raising funds. By the time he finished the one hundredth lap, Captain Tom had raised over $30 million for the NHS, with donations from all over the world. You want to talk about posterity? That is posterity, at the ripe age of one hundred—what a legacy to leave behind. Captain Tom's efforts did not go unnoticed by the British Royal Family. Not only did he get personal messages from members of the Royal Family, but the Queen knighted him (in an outdoor ceremony) at Windsor Castle.

During the publishing of this book, on January 31, 2021, Captain Tom died of COVID-19 complications. May his soul rest in peace and his legacy continue to inspire others.

I admit, the scale of Sir Captain Tom's story is an incredible feat to measure up against. But many other gestures leave me in awe. One such story is of an Italian priest, Don Giuseppe Berardelli. At the age of 72, he tested positive for COVID-19 and was going to be put on a ventilator. The world over, hospitals were seeing a shortage of ventilators due to the staggering number of infections. The priest selflessly gave up his ventilator to help a young person, who was also infected and in dire condition. Priest Berardelli paid the ultimate price, passing away in a hospital in Bergamo, Italy. To know you are giving up your chance to survive in an effort to save a young life—I hope we never lose sight of this.

Something that hit closer to home, an eleven-year-old, Ethan Reynolds from Columbus, Indiana—had a simple but effective idea. Ethan set up a table in front of his home with canned goods, protein bars, fruit, and some basic toiletries. A handwritten sign for his table read "free food" and was open for business every day, weather permitting. There were no questions asked; if you needed something from Ethan's table, you could simply help yourself. Ethan's table was frequented by mothers, kids on bicycles, homeless people, and anyone in need. This kid was in fifth grade and had such a big heart. Ethan's act of kindness had a snowball effect; others in the community routinely dropped off donations to keep the table bountiful. Kindness begets kindness. Ethan is worthy of a community impact award, wouldn't you agree?

•••

There were some much-needed, lighter moments in the news during the pandemic. The famous Shedd Aquarium in Chicago let two penguins roam free when they were on shutdown—and then proceeded to post videos and live recordings. It was cuteness overload to watch the tuxedo birds checking out the different displays. Even more adorable were the fish and other mammals who showed return interest in the penguins.

The prime minister of Norway, Erna Solberg, held a press conference for children during the COVID-19 outbreak. She answered questions submitted by kids across Norway. She was building on the Danish prime minister's idea of having a conference for kids. How amazing is that?

Speaking of kids, working from home with two toddlers was madness for us—in the beginning. Keeping peace, defusing tantrums, still attempting e-learning activities while working full-time, providing meals and snacks on-demand, sprinkled in with diaper changes and bottom wipes, was madness. I want to claim that I operated like a Hindu Goddess with multiple arms and powers to heal. But the truth is, I was more like an overwhelmed ostrich. Working from home with toddlers gave me a newfound respect for zookeepers. How do they do it? Even with just two kids, Nuwan and I felt like we were in an endless loop of keeping the monkeys fed, hydrated, and clean. And the ratio was one-to-one here.

Now imagine for a minute that it's your birthday, Diwali, Christmas, and the Fourth of July all on the same day. With the 24-7 access to me, it was like Diwali-Christmas-Ganesh and all wonderful things combined into one for Aarini! She floated from cloud nine to rainbow slides, basking in the unlimited access to *Amma* (me!). At any given point, based on whim, the moon phase, or her disposition, there were no more than six centimeters of space between us. This was regardless of my meeting schedule. Calling into meetings where I was actively participating (read: not on mute) became a tedious challenge. Nuwan and I would take turns setting the kids up with creative and fun activities in the hopes of occupying them for more than a fleeting minute. And then we'd each take our positions in the office and any other room in the house to dial into conferences. Even with all our efforts, more often than not, it sounded like I was dialing in from a fish market. Screams and squeals were exchanged on a regular basis; it was hard to tell if they were fighting or dancing.

This is how the initial couple of months went. Daycare was still open, but I couldn't dream of us working from home while choosing to send our children to preschool. If my health and exposure to a deadly virus is of enough concern that I stop going to the office, how can I be alright sending my children out?

None of this was easy, though, and work started to suffer—so we decided to hire a tutor, Linda. The extent that I could afford was three days a week for a couple of hours. But it was what we needed to take the edge off. The kids also settled into a new routine. Aarini stopped seeking me out every breathing moment, and something else magical happened. Brother and sister bonded, like they had never done before. They became allies and play buddies who pretended to fight the bad guys. Nap time was a lost battle, but the kids played so hard that bedtime became a breeze. The proud moments for me were the times Aarini reprimanded me if I uttered a disciplinary word to Vihaan in a stern tone. *She is her brother's keeper.* Watching their relationship blossom was the best thing to come out of social distancing for us.

Vihaan started online kindergarten in August of 2020, at the beginning of the school year. But around six weeks in, his kindergarten teacher, Mrs. Park, told us Vihaan was only one of two children not coming into in-person school. Based on that feedback, we decided to send him to school. Boy, if only you could have seen the difference it made to his temperament. To be in school with kids his age (sure, in a mask all day, other than while eating or drinking), forced a complete 180 in demeanor. It is so important for children—well, for all of us, but especially children—to socially interact with their peers.

As we got comfortable with Vihaan being away, we enrolled Aarini back in daycare. Both kids were out of the house, learning, interacting, playing with other little people.

•••

The pandemic, as of the time of authoring this book, has been a cruel but unique opportunity to think about empathy. It is a large-scale event that has affected everyone and caused sweeping changes to our way of life. While we are all in it together, each person's situation is in fact unique. Some have newborns whom they are caring for without help from family, due to travel restrictions. I can relate to how exhausting and sometimes scary it is to care for a newborn, always wondering if *this* cry indicates something serious. Some couples (or individuals) have grown children, and others have none. It might seem like a childless situation is more liberating during a social-distancing scenario, but it can also be isolating. I've seen married friends separate during the pressures of the pandemic, and eager-to-get pregnant couples needing to put off the next round of IVF.

Coronavirus has affected all of us. It is the extent and severity that varies. I think that realization can be fertile ground to regroup and think as a community. The pandemic has given us a chance to be better citizens.

While we still follow the directive of being socially distant, I am cautious about not being emotionally distant. Staying connected to people, expressing concern, and showing empathy are my small ways of helping others who might feel isolated. Socially distanced caring for others, writing a note, and arranging a care package are my ways of feeling connected. If you are reading this after all social distancing is lifted (wishful/hopeful/*probable?* thinking), I hope that I'm still engaging in some of these activities even when the bustle of "normal" (whatever that means) returns.

Feelings of isolation are something I'm all too familiar with from my cancer diagnosis and treatment months. I remember being surrounded by cousins and aunts, loved ones, and friends—and yet feeling so alone. That's the reason I want to do everything in my capacity to help others, while adhering to health and safety guidelines.

One of the hardest parts of social distancing for me is not being able to visit family—aging parents, newborns who made their entry into the world during a pandemic, my cousins and their children. Also, most of us are staying away from close friends and neighbors. Social distancing has felt more like social isolation, hence the extra effort *not* to be *emotionally* distant.

∙∙∙

In the midst of this pandemic, I had my regular, biannual cancer center follow-ups. Seeing my oncologists and breast surgeon are appointments I look forward to. The only other times in my life where I looked forward to seeing a doctor were during my two pregnancies. Those appointments meant that I would get to hear my babies' heartbeats—or maybe even get an ultrasound where I could see my peanuts.

I can see how strange it might sound that I like going to the cancer center. But the thing is, from the time I walk through the door, I get to see beacons of hope—starting with Debbie, the receptionist. She knows me well, we talk about her grandchild, and Debbie also met most of my family during my treatment. I love her smile; she radiates optimism. Next up, the nurses who check me in—I still know most of them. There are some who have moved on and some new faces, but I know the crux. I love seeing nurse navigator Kimmy. There's also Katie, Shannon, Annette, Kelsey, and more. I also get to see the incredible nurse practitioner, Chelsea; our children are in the same daycare. And then, finally to the celebrities: I get to spend time with Stephanie (Dr. Wagner, top MedOnc) and Kevin (don't tell me I need to remind you who this is again).

I cherish those appointments, even though they get to be fully dressed while I chill in a flimsy hospital gown. I am also thoroughly examined, which makes me feel better, like someone is watching over me. I look forward to the appointments, because I can talk to them about my concerns—certain that they won't judge me for my neurotic tendencies. At least they won't judge me to my face; I am wondering now though, what do they discuss when I leave? *That I'm fabulous, their favorite patient, such a darling, borderline insane, headstrong, petulant.....?*

Regardless, cancer center follow-ups are something I look forward to.

Having said that, my body has the complete opposite reaction to the peachy feelings I've just described. Almost always—actually *always*, without fail—my blood pressure is off the charts. I won't share the numbers with you because I don't want to alarm my cardiologist friends (Nandu and Firas, this one's for you) or family in the field, because they actually know how to interpret the numbers. Here I am confessing that the cancer center visits are cherished, but my body has a visceral, opposite response. My body betrays me. But they say mind over matter, right? So, in that vein, I don't ever cancel or reschedule my appointments. I am always on time and eager to see my care team.

The pandemic has put a damper on these appointments, though. There are no hugs. During my last appointment, my oncologists spoke to me via a mask and face shield. Stephanie and Kevin only came close while examining me, otherwise keeping a considerable distance as we spoke. These are the same people who have seen me break down, who delivered bad news—but told me they had a plan for me. These are the nurses who wrapped me with a warm blanket during chemotherapy, the pharmacists who ordered anti-nausea meds for me because I was sick to my stomach. To go to the cancer center and not be able to hug anyone is *hard*.

Something else that made matters even more isolating is that Nuwan was not allowed to be with me for the follow-ups. Most hospitals put a policy in place to limit traffic in and out of the building—patients only, no family.

Before you think I'm feeling sorry for myself, I am not. This experience—and lack of physical comfort—only heightened my concern for my core group: fellow cancer patients whom I was helping. During this time of social distancing, I am in touch with a few local women and helping another in Houston. When I say *help*, it has come down to moral support via texts and calls. I cannot go see any of these women because of the COVID risk. I had tickets booked to go help my friend in Houston, which I postponed once, then twice, and finally couldn't go at all. Normally, I like to visit the infusion center; chemotherapy sessions are long, and company is welcome. Remove me from the equation; these women can't even have their significant others with them at this time. Going to treatment alone, driving themselves, while their children are at home due to the pandemic, must be incredibly hard. I relied heavily on my family, friends, and the community for help during treatment. Without their visits and help in the kitchen while keeping the kids entertained, I don't know how I could've gotten through treatment.

My heart aches; it hurts when I think of young mothers having to do this alone.

•••

At press time for this book, no one can predict the end of the COVID-19 pandemic, yet there is hope. A few variants of the vaccine have passed the authorization and approval process around the world, and we are in a full-force vaccine drive in the U.S. Any adult in this country can now make an appointment to receive a vaccine. Logistics have been a challenge—how to ramp up vaccine production with safe and effective distribution—but I see our federal and state government, along with our local leaders, making vast strides by the day. An ongoing challenge is ensuring that people around the world receive such access.

2021 is looking a little different, and I'm sure 2022 will as well. I am optimistic that the efficacy of the vaccine will provide needed protection to people and the confidence to open shop. By the time you read this, there may already be answers to today's questions. But at this time in history as I write, I'm asking: *Will physical offices be a thing of the past? Other than production lines, will everything turn virtual?* I hope not, because I miss the camaraderie of the workplace. Being in the office provides the opportunity to network. At lunch, you run into someone you haven't worked with in ages, you share a conversation, and you think, *I need to collaborate with this individual again.* With everyone working from home, we miss out on those random run-ins.

It will also be nice to travel again. I know our first order of business will be to fly back home to Indo-Lanka and see our families.

I do wonder though if the emotional toll of the pandemic won't be so quick to reverse. As much as it is a health epidemic, it has also been a pandemic of loneliness. When we go back to an in-person office, will people shake hands? I'm going to start using the Indian *namaste*, holding my palms together. *Will we hug?* The number of hugs I got when my work colleagues and leadership heard about my cancer, or saw me in the office post-treatment . . . I kid you not, innumerable. I'm not sure how openly we will become to giving and receiving embraces again.

Then there's the mask. I, for one, will continue wearing a mask.

With so much to ponder, I'm interested to see the world post-pandemic. I hope that more than the fear and lingering isolation, the lessons in courage, innovation, patience, trust, bravado, and empathy will leave an indelible mark on the human psyche. I believe we are resilient creatures who will keep coming together in community to be stronger than we once were. *We need each other.*

13. A COMEDY OF ERRORS

"In any moment of decision, the best thing you can do is the right thing. The worst thing you can do is nothing."
—Theodore Roosevelt

My family and community have played indispensable roles in my life: my crutch when I couldn't walk, the warmth when the future seemed bleak. However, what happens when the same community lets you down? How does one reconcile that?

It was a Saturday afternoon on a bright, sunny day. I had planned an afternoon of errands—grocery shopping, mainly. After getting a trunk full of weekly produce—fruit and vegetables, poultry, fish and milk—I made my way to the Indian store. I needed the basics—curry leaves, a 10-pound bag of rice, and a similar-sized bag of wheat flour for roti. There are a few savory Indian snacks that my children love; I picked those up, too.

Now, Saturday is not an ideal day to go to the Indian store. It can get rather busy, and the store itself is small, so it feels crowded. There is only one cashier-till, and on this day, the cashier was missing, so a queue started to form. First in line was a visibly pregnant woman, masked and gloved. Bless her heart, she seemed to have done groceries in anticipation of the baby's arrival: bags full of Indian basics, mangoes, and delicacies like *kulfi*. (Kulfi is a creamy Indian ice cream, the king of ice creams. Gelato's got nothing on us.)

The Indian store has wheeled baskets for your convenience when shopping. However, once you pay for your groceries, the expectation is that you hand-carry your bags out. There is no outside shelter to deposit the baskets into.

I watched this pregnant lady doing her first run and noticed how many more runs she would need based on everything she had bought. I sized up the mango crate and thought I should help her. I looked around. Ahead of me in line was a gentleman of South Asian descent, behind me two other men—also Indian looking. They were watching the pregnant woman, but no one offered to help.

Why hasn't anyone offered to help? Where is the kindness? I approached her, at a distance of six feet or greater—and I had my mask on, of course. I said, "Excuse me, would you like a hand with your groceries?" She politely declined. I tried again, "No really, I would be happy to do it." She declined again. That's when I realized she had gloves on. With the pandemic, being pregnant must have been scary enough, and the last thing she needed was someone without gloves offering help. I took a step back and resumed my place in line.

I was seething in my spot though. *Why hasn't a single man waiting in line with nothing to do offered to help?* This is not to say pregnant women can't load their own groceries. I worked till the day before I went into labor with my firstborn. But even now, I cherish how, at the local grocery store, they used to open a checkout line just for me or offer to load my groceries when I was pregnant. I didn't *need* the help, but I appreciated being valued.

For argument's sake, let's consider that the pregnant lady had found my offer condescending. It is a possibility. But I would rather run the risk of offending someone with my act of kindness than not do anything at all. I am also OK with a rejection of my offer of help. Better a refusal to accept my assistance, than not offering help at all because a rejection would be too embarrassing.

Anyway, it was my turn, and since I didn't have much stuff, I was able to load my groceries in two runs to the car. I put the rice and flour in the back seat, since my trunk was full. I got into the driver's side, pulled out my mask, and was just about to close the door when a man blocked the door. He had a gun in his hand. I started screaming. He pressed the barrel against my chest. My heightened senses told me: *think fast, this is real, this is happening.*

The man said, "Be quiet! Be quiet!"

I stopped screaming and blurted out, "Take whatever you want."

He told me to hand over my keys. So I did. I thought he was going to take me, too. No way would I let that happen, so I slipped past the driver side door, and I ran.

I ran *for my life.*

I turned around to see if he was going to shoot me. I'm not sure why I would have wanted to know that, but checking on him was somehow my instinct. That's when I saw there was a second man who had gotten into the passenger side—his accomplice. I realized that my phone was in my purse; the purse was in the car. I had two options: run away from the scene towards the main road or run into the store where there were other people, including two friends. *Strength in numbers,* I thought—and, *someone needs to call the cops.*

When I ploughed back into the store, I started screaming, "Somebody call 911! There's a man with a gun! He is trying to steal my car!" A group of seven individuals and the cashier at checkout just stared at me.

I repeated my request.

"Can someone please give me a cell phone? I need to call 911! There are two men in my car. The guy pointed a gun at me!"

Crickets.

No one gave me their cell phone; no one called 911. From the exit door made of glass—you know, the transparent kind that you can see through—people could see two men in my car, fumbling with the key.

The cashier feebly gave me the cordless phone.

I called 911, while everyone else just stood there. Actually, that's not true; a customer at the till continued to put his groceries on the conveyer belt. An Indian lady walked in through the entry door, oblivious to the event, as I dialed 911 and told her to get away from the door.

"911, what is your emergency?"

"A man held a gun at me, and there are two men trying to steal my car. I'm at [location details]."

The 911 operator asked, "*Trying to steal your car?* Can you see them now? What are they doing?"

The men expected my car to be a push-button start, so they were looking for the key fob to put the key in and pressing random buttons on the dashboard. In their state of urgency to get away quickly with the car, the gun guy pressed the panic alarm, and the car started beeping loudly.

I'm narrating this live to the dispatcher.

"They are not able to start the car. They have the key, but they can't figure out how to turn the ignition on."

The passenger seat fellow jumped out of my car and tried to get into a Honda parked next to it. The Honda had an Indian father in the driver's seat and a child, aged seven to eight, with him. I started stepping away from their line of sight, thinking: If these guys come in, they have a gun. They can go on a rampage. They can demand for me to help them start the car, or worse, still be angry enough to use their firearm. All of these thoughts in my head meant I needed to act; *I must get out of the store.* I rushed towards the back exit, while still talking to the 911 dispatcher.

"Now they are attempting to carjack a Honda CRV that is parked next to my car."

An acquaintance asked me, "Are we better off hiding in the store?" *Finally, someone acknowledging the reality of the threat*—but note, still not doing anything about it.

I vehemently told her, "No, we need to get out." At this point, the cordless phone was out of range, and my call with 911 dropped. Can you believe in the year 2020, I am using a cordless phone to call 911?

I was out the back door. A small group had joined me in exiting, almost like they needed a leader to take action. Think of it is a slow chemical reaction when you're expecting spontaneous combustion. I said to a friend, "Ashok, may I please borrow your cell phone? My phone is in the car, and I need to talk to 911." Ashok gave me his phone but forgot to unlock it. I returned it to him with a request to unlock.

If you're wondering why I am going into such excruciating detail, it is to illustrate how many precious minutes were lost in inaction. Inaction of others.

Back on my call. "Are you sending someone? I don't know where the men are."

Ashok chimed in that he saw one of the guys run away from the scene, towards the gas station.

I told the operator that.

The dispatcher told me that a police officer should be there any second and asked if my car was still there.

I told him, "I don't know, because I'm not in a location where I can see my vehicle. The car is a VW Tiguan with license plates XYZ." *That's right. In a moment of complete panic, I am still able to relay relevant information.*

A cop finally came, seven minutes from the time the gun was pressed against my chest. Seven minutes of dread. The sight of the cop car was the first time I felt like I was going to be OK. I could finally reassure myself, it is safe now.

My whole body physically shook as I narrated the incident with as much detail as I could recall. The officer headed towards the front of the grocery store; I followed several feet behind him. Even though Ashok reported that the criminals ran, and others corroborated the same, I didn't know if they were hiding out. Plus, I thought, we have only one officer; the gun ratio is still 1:1.

It truly appeared that they had taken off, so I joined the police officer. The two men failed in their attempt at carjacking, twice over. The Honda and my car were still in the parking lot. Moreover, my key was on the driver's side floor mat. They couldn't figure out that mine was an analog key, no keyless start, and in the urgency of their escape, they dropped the key in the car and ran.

They didn't take my car, my purse, or my phone. They panicked and ran.

A second police officer got to the scene of the crime. He took a recorded statement from me. They also said a detective was on his way to collect DNA samples. There was now a small crowd of Indian/South Asian men and women waiting to hear what happened—some of whom were the exact people who had heard me screaming, "Somebody call 911!"

After I was done giving my statement, I went to speak to Honda dude. He told me he had seen the two men fumbling with the key, pushing random buttons. I was flabbergasted. *Why didn't he hit the gas and get away from the scene?* You know me by now; I can be rather direct. I didn't keep that thought to myself and asked him point-blank, "When you saw two men attacking my car, you were parked right next to me, and you have a child in the car with you. Why didn't you just take off?"

When his response was something around "putting his seat belt on," I tuned him out. It was asinine; he had a child with him. He should've hit the pedal and fled.

I needed to call Nuwan, so I asked Ashok if I could use his phone to call my husband. Nuwan picked up the call from an unknown number. "Honey, it's me. I'm OK; I'm not hurt." Nuwan was distraught; he must've thought I was in a wreck. He was shocked when he heard what had happened.

"I'll be home once the detective gets samples for fingerprints and DNA," I told him.

"I want to be there with you," Nuwan insisted. "The kids and I will leave right away."

There is no way I would allow my children into the scene of a fresh crime. "Absolutely not," I told him. "The kids are to stay at home where it is safe." Nuwan obliged, although I know he was worried about me and wished he could be on the scene.

While I was waiting for the detective to arrive, I got chatting with the officers. One of the officers said, "We don't come across car jackings in Columbus that often." They were, themselves, surprised at the turn of events.

The tension of the incident slowly began to subside. I began to feel like myself again. I told the officers, "I am a cancer survivor, two years in remission." Then I added, "If cancer wasn't going to kill me, I sure wasn't going to let a dimwit with a gun take my life." They had sympathetic smiles and said kind words congratulating me for being in remission. One of the officers shared a story about two loved ones in his family being breast cancer survivors as well.

About two hours after the ordeal, I was released to go home. I got in my car and drove back. Nuwan was in the driveway with the kids waiting for me.

We hugged.

• • •

Several thoughts went through my mind in the days following the incident, including: *how did this happen in broad daylight, in the middle of day, in a busy parking lot?* Another friend who had been at the store, Yogesh, and I had discussed the incident while the cops were still around. He said, pointing to his car in the corner of the lot, "Look at where my car is parked, in an isolated location away from other cars. Your car is right by the exit door, in a prime, ideal spot for easily loading groceries. Why did they go for your car?" It was a rhetorical question, but it got me thinking. *Why did they target me?* They would rather hedge their bets on carjacking a petite woman parked right under the CCTV camera, than go for a car at the far end of the lot where the owner is male.

That reminded me, the store had a security camera by the door. I was hoping the detective could see the footage and find identifying features of the perpetrators. But as luck would have it, the CCTV wasn't turned on.

This attempted carjacking also made me think of the pregnant lady. Thank God they didn't go for her; she was the most vulnerable.

My mind wandered to the collective inaction of everyone at the scene. The cashier didn't lock the doors, and no one thought of barricading the door in order to stop the men from entering. No one had the confidence to call 911. No one used their cell phone to get a picture or video of the men, who were clearly visible from the shoppers' and cashiers' vantage points. Some even continued their grocery shopping!

Since that day, I have run through this scenario multiple times, and my hypothesis on inaction has run the gamut. Was it that . . . everyone froze, or they didn't believe a hysterical woman? Did they lack the confidence to speak to police, or was it that they couldn't be bothered to call 911 . . . Saturday night dinner plans and all? Was it because they didn't want to be a witness to a crime, then dragged into the investigation?

I get that human beings have a fight, flight, or freeze response to imminent threat. But I can't get my head around everyone freezing; not a single human stepped up. I shudder to think if this was due to a lack of empathy.

To further make my point, think of the pregnant woman doing multiple rounds to her car to load her shopping, while nobody offered help.

In a conversation about this situation with Gary, he aptly asked, "How do you teach empathy?" I take that as a challenge. How *do* you teach empathy?

I started researching empathy online. Most examples I found were geared towards children's education. Rightfully so, empathy is something that needs to be ingrained into children. A simple example of how we teach our kids about empathy, "How would you feel if Maxwell took away *your* toy?" Empathy starts with learning to put yourself in someone else's shoes, to think about the other person's perspective. We are not necessarily born with it, but we learn about it in social settings, or our suffering makes us cognizant of others' suffering. I realize empathy exists on a spectrum and everyone may not feel the same level of empathy for others in a given situation. In any case, being able to see another perspective remains key.

I struggled to explain the lack of empathy in that store on that fateful Saturday.

Somewhere along the journey from interdependent communities and extended family living together to modern-day society, which is self-reliant and self-centered, some of us have lost sight of empathy. The basis of human existence is compassion. In a life-threatening incident involving a firearm, where was the unity? Every single person in that store was Indian. Which makes me ponder. I am proud of where I come from and my Indian heritage . . . but I'm not quite sure where we're headed.

I spent some time contemplating our relationship with police back in India. The local, everyday, no-power cops in India are undervalued and unprotected. On a good day, they may carry a baton for protection, but most do not have access to a firearm. These officers come from lower-middle-class or low-income homes. Their job isn't easy by any means. But then there is corruption—corrupt cops who accept bribes, power-hungry ones who trade favors, and occasionally a drunk-with-power cop who rapes a woman in distress when she approaches him for protection. Given this context, Indians fear harassment—and sometimes physical harm—from law enforcement.

The absence of empathy breeds *apathy*. And my fear is that apathy brings about the decline of humanity. This is already happening in the dark corners of the world. Consider a brutal rape in Delhi, where the victim lay naked on the side of a busy road for hours before passersby called the police. In another situation, a teenager from southern India was hit by a bus. People huddled around him to take pictures. No one helped, and he bled to death.

On a personal note, an Indian friend, Rahul, told me about the time his parents were in a car crash. A passerby approached them. His parents assumed it was to help, but instead the man stole their wallet, purse, and possessions.

I want to bury my head in the sand and pretend that such incidents of bystander inaction are rare. But I can't. I have read about similar such instances of theft at the site of a crash. This amalgamation of apathy and shrewd opportunity makes me feel helpless at times. My Saturday afternoon rendezvous with carjackers—*did my homies feel apathy, since that is what we saw growing up?*

In contrast to what we might have read, seen, or experienced in India, shootings have sadly become commonplace in the U.S. Businesses and workplaces here train employees on armed-aggressor response. My office has mandatory training on these topics, on a recurrent basis. Schools, too, practice the active shooter drill. My son and kids as young as five are made to recite, "In case of emergency, call 911." The young task force is then educated on what is an emergency that warrants reporting: if they see a fire, if someone passes out, if they witness a crime, if they are in a car crash or witness one. With this culture and emphatic message on the importance of reporting an emergency, I grapple with what happened that day.

•••

There are times when your personal, dire situation and anguish can make you less empathetic. It's normal to have phases where we are so wrapped up in our own trauma or issue that we can't easily see outside of ourselves to help others. I am guilty of that lack of compassion.

Less than a year into remission, I was helping a teammate deal with the failing health of her . . . dog. I tried to provide emotional support, but instead I felt a bit detached and emotionally distant from sorrow of this sort. The worst part is that I love dogs; Nuwan and I grew up with dogs, and we plan to have canines in our home once Vihaan and Aarini are housebroken. My muddled sense of compassion left me ashamed, but my heart kept saying: you think *this* is tough?

I know that was unfair of me, and often I need to remind myself to refrain from participating in the "grief Olympics"—you know, the rabbit hole of "mine is worse than yours" when comparing sorrow. Since then, I have conscientiously worked, and continue to work on, my empathy meter.

Days and weeks after the attempted carjacking incident, I developed bitterness toward the bystanders and store workers. About a month after the incident, a friend told me he was at the store and he asked the cashier about the incident. The cashier denied any knowledge of the episode. I was let down by my community, and that festered. I felt marginalized by the whole thing. In the stereotypically Indian fashion, no one wanted to talk about an uncomfortable topic—something I am all too familiar with.

I believe empathy can be taught. We are told empathy *should* be taught to our children, so we instruct them on how to be kind to others and put themselves in their friends' shoes. Empathy is a coveted quality in leaders. Empathetic leaders build high performing teams. At the risk of losing sight of empathy—at the risk of succumbing to the bystander effect—I propose that we need to *practice* empathy like any other healthy habit. Eat your vegetables, exercise your body, care for your mental well-being—and practice empathy.

In a way, most of our good habits are self-serving. We do them for our personal welfare—for our physical and psychological health.

Empathy, on the other hand, is for the greater good. And there is unmatched gratification when we do something for others, even if our contribution is as humble as lending a listening ear or being the hero of someone else's story by calling 911.

14. STUBBORN HOPE

"Magic happens when you don't give up, even when you want to. The universe always falls in love with a stubborn heart."
—J.M. Storm

Before I was diagnosed, I thought of life as binary. That's what engineers do; we think in ones and zeros. In any given situation, I tend toward all-or-nothing.

During treatment, I craved black-and-white solutions; but medicine and the human body don't work that way. My disease was a struggle, but the light at the end of the tunnel was that after treatment, I would start a new, post-cancer life. Only after going through the journey did I realize there is no reset button, at least not for me. The best I can do is re-center and relearn.

I needed to learn how to be whole again—in mind and body. My body was irrevocably different, and my mind had its own issues to work through. But the journey did teach me something valuable—a lesson in hope.

Hope offers buoyancy. Regardless of how dire the situation is, hope keeps your head above water. Hope, by definition, is stubborn—because it does not follow logic or sound argument. It is one of those against-all-odds feelings that comes to fruition.

Just to be clear, hope is *not* optimism. I look at optimism as a glass half full. Hope is knowing that the glass is half empty and using your acumen to redesign the glass. Hope is the conviction that misfortune can be endured. For me, hope was trust—trust that my cancer care team had developed the best treatment plan for my disease, and that I was on the path to permanent remission.

We don't say cure when it comes to cancer; it's remission. Calling it *permanent remission*, now that is hope.

Through my cancer journey, I realized that hope, like faith, should not be blind. When I was given my treatment plan, I sought a second and third opinion to bolster my confidence in my care team. Hope involves being realistic about the hardship you're facing, while devising a way out. And there might be several ways out, so you need to evaluate your options. The peddlers of positivity are uncomfortable using fear and uncertainty in their vocabulary. But it is in the depths of uncertainty that hope shines brightest.

Hope is the feeling I got when I connected with young women who had endured my type of cancer. Their struggle gave me the courage to accept my struggle. The realization that I wasn't alone was half the battle. To see that others had walked this path and come out the other side gave me strength.

I want to be that beacon for others starting their battles.

My desire for the foreseeable future is that we make strides in cancer treatment. The first thing I wish we could do is improve chemotherapy.

My oncologist, Stephanie, told us that chemotherapy is on the brink of change, with less toxic modalities and drugs that are temperature dependent. The dosage and precision in delivery will go a long way in improving the patient's overall experience, energy, and both short- and long-term side effects.

As much I want chemotherapy to go down as easy as a vitamin supplement, I know we need to start at the root with early and accurate detection. Today we have ultrasounds, mammograms, biopsies, CT scans, MRIs, and PET scans as some of the options to determine the staging and grade of cancer. This classification then dictates the course of treatment. These crucial scans give us an idea of how much the disease has spread.

The medical community has come a long way, but we need even better, more accurate, less invasive forms of detection. My radiation oncologist told me about a new ultrasound technology that can supersede mammogram technology. It is good at eliminating the noise factors that mammograms cannot distinguish between. And this form of scan is not as painful and awkward as the mammogram. Early and accurate detection is really where we should start the fight.

Something that confuses me about cancer is when adults with familial cancer, young adults with low-risk behavior, adolescents and children, are diagnosed but turn out negative for genetic mutations. Sure, we can assume it's chance and coincidence. That is what I was told: life dealt me a crappy hand. But I question: is it chance, environmental factors, genetics, or a combination of all three?

With environmental factors, I do wonder, is it the water we are drinking with the contaminants in America, the air we breathe in Asia, or the food we eat? With each situation, Nuwan pointed out that there is a catalyst— such as water, pollutants, and food. But then there must be genes that trigger the reaction, the onset of cancer. In the absence of that logic, every person drinking contaminated water, breathing polluted air, or eating pesticide-coated food would get cancer. But that's not how cancer works. Genetic differences or triggers must be the differentiating factor.

Given this philosophy, I have my eye on genetic research. Most of us have heard about the BRCA gene mutation known to increase the risk of female cancers, but there is much to uncover here. Identifying *all* of the gene mutations associated with cancer will help our understanding of what needs to be fixed. I realize using superlatives in the goal of mapping the human body is a behemoth ask. But we should challenge ourselves with the impossible, like human beings have done throughout history.

Science gives me hope.

Which takes me to something that seems straight out of science fiction, called CRISPR, pronounced crisper. If you haven't geeked out on science podcasts, CRISPR stands for **c**lustered **r**egularly **i**nterspaced **s**hort **p**alindromic **r**epeats. Rolls right off the tongue, right? CRISPR is a genome editing tool. Commonly known as (commonly in the field of genetics and geekdom) CRISPR Cas9, CRISPRs are special strands of DNA, while Cas9 is a protein that is capable of cutting the DNA. The molecular scissors, as they say, can cut strands of DNA at a targeted location in the genome so that bits of DNA can be added or removed. If this doesn't sound like science fiction to you, you must be a geneticist. Because the first time I heard about CRISPR, I thought, why aren't more people talking about this?

Apparently, CRISPR has been used in food and agriculture. Biochemists and the like are on a quest to discover how CRISPR can be used to fight diseases like cancer. CRISPR-edited immune cells can be an effective line of defense in hunting down cancer cells and using our own immune system to fight them. The dream is that all the progress made so far in immunotherapy will result in making chemotherapy totally unnecessary.

How amazing would that be, to attack cancer cells with our own immune systems? We are so close. I want to be able to talk about, "Back in the day, we used chemotherapy…"

With anything this powerful, there will always be ethical dilemmas. I'm thinking of designer babies, taller-stronger-blonder-better, and my point of contention: a preferred baby sex of boy.

But here's where my glass half full comes into being: I have faith. I have faith in humanity—that we will use genetic research and therapies for the right reasons. Maybe that faith is naïve, but after the hardship I have put my family through, I would like to own this naiveté.

There can be no hope without naiveté. For instance, in the depths of my hopelessness, my cousin, Catharine, said to me, "Even if there is a one percent chance of survival, Niyati, you are that one percent, no doubt." Catharine's love and conviction for me instilled hope in my future. And she made her statement unqualified, but I still remember the reassurance it provided me.

In 2020, while I was helping a young Indian mother battling breast cancer with an unfavorable prognosis, I said, "I am going to tell you what my cousin, Catharine, said to me. 'If there is a one percent chance of survival, you will be that one percent.' Vedika, you are that one percent." Upon hearing this, she started crying. She said she yearned for her cancer care team to say that to her. I tried to console her. But my loyalties still lay with the cancer care team; they cannot not dispense unverifiable assurances, as they see death on the regular. But I reap the benefits of stubborn hope. So, unreserved, I could claim to Vedika that she would survive cancer.

Hope is contagious—*highly* contagious, might I add. Even in dire situations—disease, poverty, war, and genocide—when a few possess hope, others cling to it. Warranted or not, hope enables people to pull through during adversity. It drives my passion for helping young breast cancer patients. I want these survivor sisters to see me and realize their future. I was a bald, moonfaced, pale mother who chose breast amputation. Today, I share Diwali cards with cancer patients and go to the infusion center to represent. *If I made it, so can you.*

That's another thing I say often to recently diagnosed women who think I'm brave or have done something extraordinary to make it to the other side of treatment. I didn't. I endured in the same way the treatment will demand suffering from them. I went through the motions, collected my scars, left a part of me behind, and emerged on the other side—as will they. And with complete conviction, I remind anyone who has been touched by cancer: *if I can do this, you can, too.*

You can call me the broker of mad hope.

•••

A source of hope I hold onto dearly is the future generation, our children. I look at the new generation—youth who are enthusiastic, optimistic, and ready to solve complex problems. I know that traditionally, each generation laments the decline of the present generation of youth. As the joke goes, "When I was your age, I walked uphill to school, both ways," to illustrate how much easier life has become. But this time around, we might end up relying on them more than prior generations did with their offspring. Kids today are taught at preschool to use words to describe emotions—and that sorrow is acceptable, crying doesn't emasculate. Boys and girls can emote, and they are gauged on emotional intelligence as much as on fine motor skills and spatial awareness. These practices will raise a generation comfortable with vulnerability—and leaders who can pick up on and influence the emotions of those around them.

Children today are exposed to reality and challenges at an early age. They are taught facts about climate change and have already lived through a pandemic. They have an acute sense of responsibility; just take eleven-year-old Ethan and his table of generosity as an example.

Call me green, but I believe we are raising a generation that will change the world—for the better.

As for me, I have big plans. If you can't sense the sarcasm in that statement, you don't know me at all. My big plan is to make it to forty. Unlike women dreading the big 4-0 or worrying about when menopause will descend, I am excited about turning forty. My fortieth birthday will mark five years in remission. In the biz, it is considered an important milestone, because the chances of recurrence drop drastically on the other side of it. It is also another occasion for me to ring the survivor's bell.

It's funny how the definition of age changes after cancer. Old age is a privilege, and I want the luxury of complaining about grey hairs.

Other than my glorious plan for aging, I continue my quest to destigmatize cancer. That is a big part of my calling. In the two years since publishing my first book and giving my TEDx talk, my name has been circulated in the Indian darknet.

Is the Indian darknet a network that circulates illicit substances, you ask? No. It's worse. It is a community that knows about my disease but is too uncomfortable to say, "breast cancer." It is a segment of people who need help but cannot ask their own family, so they reach out to me, a stranger. It is a group that only talks about the c-word in whispers, but knows I'm the brash one who talks about it openly. I am an *infamous* woman whom the darknet mentions, but few homies would acknowledges in public. As a result, I randomly get contacted by Indian women who have recently been diagnosed. It is my honor to assist them. I listen, empathize, coach, and mentor. I encourage these women to ask the tough questions—to be advocates for themselves. For I can relate; I've been there, and it wasn't easy. It is my God-given opportunity to serve the community and help others through their journey. And if I can make a sister laugh in the process, I call it a slam dunk.

The thing is any given society is marred by taboos. Let's consider infertility and miscarriage, separation, divorce, sexual orientation, mental health, addiction . . . the list is long. Eradicating these taboos starts with my step one—destigmatizing *it*. Whatever "it" might mean to you. The barrier we face in having an honest conversation is our aversion to vulnerability. We shy away from difficult conversations, because they require us to be true to our feelings, address our fears, and emote. We want to appear strong and impenetrable. Our pre-programmed perception of vulnerability—that chink in our armor—taints our understanding.

I challenge you to change that perception. Showing your humanity is strength; owning your struggles is courage; to say in the present tense, not after the fact, "I need help," is bloody brave.

Unabashed, I ask you to find, or better yet *build*, a platform where you can tackle stigma. I want you to wear vulnerability as your purple heart—and exercise empathy as a muscle you've beefed up in your last mental gymnastics. Be your own biggest advocate.

And while you're in the process of becoming unabashed, I ask you to be a champion for the voiceless.

DISCUSSION GUIDE

You're invited to enhance your book club, support group, or gathering of friends with this discussion guide. This page may be reproduced and shared for these educational purposes only. (Copyright applies to the rest of the book.)

Q1: The author talks about the pioneers in her family, a piece of her legacy that she is recording and wants to share with her children. What is the ancestral narrative you would like to share with your book club members?

Q2: What are your thoughts about the author's suggestion that children should wear uniforms to school?

Q3: *Legislative inertia* is a scenario wherein institutional forces make the updating of laws a daunting task. This has left some outdated laws in place. Are there any such laws you're aware of that may affect you or those you care about?

Q4: What are your thoughts about the incident at the grocery store? What do you think caused the collective inaction of bystanders?

Q5: The author briefly mentions *embryonic lottery*, an acknowledgement that where you are born, your race, and your socioeconomic status are factors of chance. Discuss what this term means to you.

Q6: How has the COVID-19 pandemic affected you?

Q7: Did the *gender parity hierarchy of needs* speak to you? Are there tiers you would add, remove, or revise?

Q8: What do you think about the author's fascination with the cosmos? Do you share this fascination? Why or why not?

Q9: The author mentioned the importance of hope. What does hope look like to you, in your life or the life of someone you know?

Q10: What do you think are some acts that best display empathy to others?

Q11: Do you think we are preparing our next generation to show more compassion and empathy? How can we contribute to this process?

Q12: Never judge a book by its cover, but seriously, what did you think of the cover of this book?

Q13: If you could ask the author one question, what would it be? The author can be reached at www.columbusauthor.com

ACKNOWLEDGEMENTS

Husband, father, better half, the ying to my bang (not a typo) Nuwan: This work of honesty wouldn't have come to fruition without your love, patience, and encouragement.

My sister Priya and brother-in-law Kamlesh: May our four children be blessed with the closeness, loyalty, and affection that we enjoy in each other. Thank you for being my fiercest supporters.

Karen Ramsey-Idem, Archita Fritz, Jennifer Borland, Anastasia Ustinova and Dr. Weiss: You were my beta readers, the first people outside of immediate family to lay eyes on the manuscript and provide a blurb. In the absence of a powerhouse publishing company, I relied on you to loan me your voice and title. Thank you for the constructive criticism and giving my book clout. Unabashed is a better read because of you.

Jocelyn Carbonara: You've gone above and beyond your editorial task to make a personal connection with me. Your input has helped morph this book into a poignant essay.

Gary Johansen, Kevin McMullen: You had my back as I discovered how beautiful and messy survivorship can be, for that I thank you.

Vikram dada: You are the only person I don't need to write a paragraph for but will still know how much you mean to me.

AUTHOR BIO

Niyati Tamaskar is a mother, engineer, entrepreneur, public speaker, and author. Her memoir, *Unafraid: A Survivor's Quest for Human Connection*, was featured in *Forbes* magazine as one of eight books that spark human connection.

Niyati speaks on issues of cultural bias, the stigma of cancer, and more. Her speaking and media appearances include her signature TEDx talk, a cover and feature spread in *Columbus* magazine on her journey and message of destigmatizing cancer, and a video created by Breastcancer.org on "How Niyati Tamaskar Overcame Cultural Cancer Stigma to Become an Advocate"—aimed at highlighting the minority experience while facing cancer.

Niyati lives in Indiana with her husband and their two children. Her hobbies include cooking and enjoying the great outdoors.

www.ingramcontent.com/pod-product-compliance
Lightning Source LLC
LaVergne TN
LVHW051519070426
835507LV00023B/3196